TEN GIRLS
WHO MADE
A DIFFERENCE

TEN GIRLS
WHO MADE
A DIFFERENCE

LIGHT KEEPERS

Irene Howat

CF4•K

For Hilda

© copyright 2002 Christian Focus Publications
Reprinted 2003, 2004, 2005 twice and 2007
ISBN: 978-1-85792-776-4

Published by Christian Focus Publications Ltd,
Geanies House, Fearn, Tain, Ross-shire,
IV20 1TW, Scotland, Great Britain.
www.christianfocus.com
email:info@christianfocus.com

Cover design by Alister Macinnes
Cover illustration by Elena Temporin
Milan Illustrations Agency
Printed and bound in Denmark
by Nørhaven Paperback A/S.

All incidents retold in these stories are based on true situations. Where specific information about childhood incidents has been unobtainable the author has written these paragraphs using other information concerning family life, hobbies, home life, relationships freely available in other biographies.

Cover illustration depicts Maria Dyer (who became Maria Taylor, wife of Hudson Taylor but a missionary in her own right). She is leaving China to go to England with her sister. Both girls were being sent back to England to complete their education. However Maria returned to China some years later to start her own mission work and subsequently met Hudson Taylor and they fell in love.

Contents

Monica of Thagaste

Monica wiped her parched lips. 'I'm so thirsty,' she said. 'May I have some water?'

'You'll have water at dinner-time,' the maid told her. 'Move into the shade and you'll not feel so dry.'

The girl licked her lips. There was no point in arguing. As she couldn't be bothered getting to her feet in the heat, she crawled the short distance to the shade of a wall.

'You'll get your clothes in a mess if you do that,' the maid told her. But before the woman could do anything else, Monica distracted her in the way she knew always worked. 'Tell me a story of when you were young,' she begged.

'I'll tell you something about the history of this town. A girl should know about the place she comes from.'

'What are you going to tell me?' Monica asked.

'Thagaste, as you know, has about 2000 people living in it,' the maid began. 'When I was young it wasn't nearly as big. But the Romans were still in charge. I loved watching the Roman soldiers marching. And I never heard one of them complain about needing a drink, no matter how hot it was in the sun,' she said, looking at the girl pointedly. 'There were all kinds of things to see and do. But one thing I didn't like was the slave market. I once saw a couple with three children for sale. The parents were sold to one man and the children sold separately to three others. I've never forgotten that mother's cries as she was dragged away, or the look on her husband's face.'

'Where did the children go?' Monica asked.

'They were bought by traders on their way to the Mediterranean coast. They were probably sent to Italy.'

'Is that far away?' she asked.

'It's about two days' journey to the sea from here, then I don't know how far across the water,' said the maid. 'But you can be sure they would never see their parents again.'

'Slavery's cruel,' Monica said. The maid didn't comment as she wasn't a free woman. 'Go on,' the girl urged, wanting to hear more.

'Well,' said the maid, 'when I was twelve I went to work for your grandmother. I'd heard strange stories about Christians but she was the first one I really knew. You don't remember her, but she was one of the best people who ever lived. She loved the Lord Jesus with all her heart. At first I thought that was odd because Jesus had died about 250 years before that. I couldn't understand how anyone could worship a man who had died when we had all the Roman gods to worship. But your grandmother told me that Jesus died on the cross to take away my sins. It was through her I became a Christian. It was also because of what he learned from his mother that your father became a believer too.'

'It's time for dinner,' a voice called from the house.

'Thank goodness for that,' Monica said, 'I'm so thirsty I could drink the whole Mediterranean Sea!'

'I think you'd be even thirstier if you tried that!' laughed the maid.

The girl looked puzzled. 'Why?' she demanded.

'Because the seas are full of salty water,' her companion explained.

Monica looked at the old woman. 'Rubbish!' she said, and ran into the house for her dinner and a long drink. After her first glass of water she asked for another. 'You're thirsty today,' her father said. Monica

9

started to giggle. 'Tell us all the joke,' he said. The girl repeated what her maid had said about salt water in the sea, though she could hardly do so for laughing.

'What did you say when she told you that?' her dad asked.

'I told her it was rubbish!' giggled the girl.

'Well, you were wrong and she was right. And as soon as you've eaten you'll go and apologise.'

'But Father, she's just a maid!'

'Don't you ever say that again,' he demanded. 'She may be a maid but she's also a child of God.'

'Why don't you let me drink water between meals?' Monica asked the maid the following afternoon.

'If you drank on and off all day you'd get into the habit of it. That's all very well now when all you drink is water and milk, but think what a state you'd get into when you're grown up and able to drink wine.'

'I promise I won't,' Monica pled.

The maid shook her head. 'I'm not taking any chances.'

'Could you bring some wine up from the cellar?' Monica's father asked, some months later. Monica ran to do what he asked.

Taking some wine from a cask she poured it into a flagon.

'What does it taste like?' she wondered.

When the flagon was full she lifted it to her lips, sniffed, and took a tiny mouthful. 'It tastes funny,' she told the young maid who was with her, before coughing and spluttering as she swallowed. The maid wasn't at all pleased.

Monica couldn't wait for the next day when she could take another little drop. However, as the days passed the little drops became bigger. It wasn't long before Monica was drinking quite a lot of her father's wine.

'Please don't drink any more,' the young maid said one day as they went into the cellar together.

'What's it got to do with you?' Monica demanded.

'It's not good for you,' the other girl explained. 'And, apart from that, when your father discovers his wine is going missing he'll think I've been stealing it and drinking it myself.'

'It would serve you right!' spat Monica. 'Who do you think you are speaking to me like that? I could have you sold!'

The maid felt as though she'd been punched. But she couldn't stop herself replying. 'You're just an alcoholic,' she said. 'Every time you come down you take a drink. You can't help yourself. You're just an alcoholic!'

Monica's anger rose. But instead of hitting the maid what the maid had said hit out at her. A lesson was learned in the cellar that day.

'I've found a husband for you,' Monica's father told her some years later. 'Patricius is a decent man and he'll make a good husband.'

'But he's not a Christian,' the girl said, for by then she was a believer.

'Well it's up to you to be such a godly wife that he'll want to become one,' she was told.

That's exactly what Monica tried to do, though her mother-in-law didn't make things easy. Patricius was not the best of husbands, but Monica lived at peace with him and was a fine mother to their children.

'When I was a girl,' she told her son Augustine, 'we had a maid from whom I learned such a lot.'

'What did she teach you?' the boy asked, hoping she'd tell him once again the story of the salty seawater. That was one of his favourites.

'She told me the stories of Jesus,' Monica

said, 'about him feeding great crowds of people, about him walking on the water and healing people who were sick and blind and deaf and those who had leprosy too.'

'Nonsense!' scoffed Patricius, who was just passing by, 'your god can't heal lepers any more than the Roman gods can.' He laughed. 'Don't believe all your mother tells you,' he said, slapping the boy on the back. 'Half of what she says is fairy stories.'

Without saying anything to disagree Monica rose and went into the house. When Augustine followed her he found his mother on her knees praying for her husband and children.

'The boy's badly ill,' Patricius said, as he left their home with two chickens dangling from his hand.

'Where are you going?' Monica asked.

'I'm going to sacrifice these to the gods and ask them to make him better. Instead of just praying you should sacrifice something to your god too,' he snapped as he left.

Augustine moaned with the pain in his stomach. 'Will you make a sacrifice, Mum?' he asked.

'I don't need to, son,' she said. 'Jesus made all the sacrifice that will ever be needed when he died on the cross.' She knelt beside him, praying that he'd get better.

Augustine believed he was dying and thought about becoming a Christian. But he made an amazing recovery and decided not to bother. 'There will be plenty of time when I grow up,' he thought.

'Where is she?' yelled Patricius, as he came near his home.

'Mum's praying,' replied Augustine, who was now a boy in his teens.

'Poor woman!' the man laughed. 'For years she's been praying for you to become a Christian but you've become just like your dad; you know a pretty girl when you meet one. No wonder your mother's at her prayers.'

Monica heard what was said. 'Lord Jesus,' she prayed. 'Please may the boy become a Christian. Do whatever you need to do to make him realise that he needs his sins forgiven.'

'Will you not trust in Jesus?' she asked Augustine, when she rose from her knees.

'One day,' he said, 'but not yet.'

It wasn't easy for Monica to watch the life her son led. He didn't pay much attention to anything she'd taught him. But this made her pray all the more for his conversion, especially after he went off to study in Carthage and then when he left Africa in 383 on his way to Italy. Not long after Monica followed him there.

'How long will it be till he comes to faith?' she asked God, over and over and over again. 'Please make it soon. Please don't let him get into an even bigger mess than he's in just now.'

On the outside it seemed that Augustine was doing well because he was a very clever man, but he still led an immoral life that hurt his mum terribly. Every time they talked about Christianity he said the same thing, 'One day, but not yet.'

When Augustine was thirty-two years old he knew in himself he couldn't go on the way he was.

'When I was going along the street today,' he once told Monica, 'I saw a beggar laughing and I thought to myself he has nothing and I have everything but he's happier than I am.'

Monica's heart filled with hope. Was Augustine finally thinking seriously about life? How delighted she was when he started going to church occasionally.

'Where are you two off to?' Monica asked Augustine and his friend one day.

'Just out to the garden,' they said. She

noticed they had a book with them. It was some time before the men came in, and when they did she saw her son's face. He was smiling as he'd not smiled for years. His eyes shone and he threw his arms around her.

'I was in the garden and I heard a child's voice saying "Take it up and read it." At first I thought it was a nursery rhyme but then I realised it was God telling me to read the Bible. I opened this and read where it opened.' He held up the Bible book of Romans. 'It spoke right to me, telling me that I had to look to Jesus and leave my immoral life behind. And suddenly I knew it was true, that what you'd told me all these years was true!' Monica's heart was singing. 'I'm a Christian, Mum. Your prayers are answered.'

Augustine and Monica planned to leave Italy and go back to North Africa but she died before they could leave. It didn't matter that she never knew her son became the most famous Christian of his day, one of the most famous Christians of all time. All that mattered to Monica was that her prayers had been answered - Augustine was a child of God and she would see him again in the Kingdom of Heaven.

Fact File: The Romans. In the ancient world Roman was the name given to the dominant people of the country we now call Italy. Many centuries before Christ's birth these people settled in a village called Rome beside the River Tiber. They gradually came to rule the whole of Italy and eventually the empire became one of the greatest the world has ever seen.

 Keynote: Monica's life was very different to yours or mine. Not many people today have a maid but Monica's family had several. Monica, however, had to learn respect for the people who worked for her family. Monica's father reminded her that her maid was also a child of God. Being a child of God means that you are part of the royal family of heaven - sons and daughters of the one true God. To be a child of God you must love and follow the Lord Jesus Christ.

Think: Monica had been warned that alcohol could have a bad effect on her life if she took too much of it. But she didn't listen to the warning and experimented anyway. It is easy to fall into bad and life-threatening habits such as drinking alcohol and taking drugs. Pray to God that he will protect you and that he will give you the strength to say no to sin.

Prayer: Lord Jesus, thank you for dying on the cross to save your people from their sins. Help me to lead a life that pleases you. Protect me from the danger of sin. If people try to persuade me to take drugs, drink or behave in a way that is against your law, help me to say no. Give me the strength to honour you with my life. Amen.

Katherine Luther

'Catch it if you can!' Katherine threw the wooden ball in the air. She was standing in a circle of girls, all with their eyes shut and their hands beating the air like windmills as they tried to catch the ball that might be coming in their direction. 'Missed!' Katherine yelled, delighted. If they all missed just twice more she had won the game. And she really wanted to win because she really wanted the prize. The girls formed a circle again and waited. Katherine stood in the middle, twirled round and round then threw the ball. 'Catch it if you can!' Again twelve arms circled in the air, and once again no one caught it. 'Last time!' the delighted child said. 'And if nobody catches it you've each got to go to Sister Mary's garden and bring me back a strawberry!'

Eyes were closed tight and hands held out all round the circle. The ten-year-old spun round and round then round again. 'Catch it if you can!' A dozen arms spun this way and that. 'Gotcha!' called out one. But the ball fell from her grasp and landed with a thud on the grass. Katherine von Bora clapped her hands with excitement. 'Now you've each got to get me a strawberry! But watch out that Sister Mary doesn't catch you.'

Katherine looked for a place where she could eat her strawberries in peace. There was no point in going to the schoolroom because the nun who taught them would still be tidying up. And the nun who milked the convent cow would be in the dairy. 'I know!' Katherine decided. 'I'll go to the orchard and climb an apple tree. The nuns won't see me there and I can whisper down to the girls when they walk by.'

She chose a tree near the path that ran between the garden and the first convent building. Then she hitched her long dress up, tucking the hem into her belt, and climbed up into the shade of the leaves. 'Here they come!' she said to herself, as her guilty-looking friends appeared from behind the garden gate. 'Psst!' she whispered, when they passed underneath her. 'I'm up here.'

'Come down, you clown!' one girl said. 'No, you come up with my strawberries.' The girls checked that the coast was clear then one by one climbed up the tree beside Katherine. She was so pleased with herself that she shared the strawberries out between them.

'Where are those girls?' It was Sister Mary, and she was walking through the orchard!

'Sh,' Katherine warned. 'Don't even breathe!' The nun passed underneath the very tree they were in as she went to the garden in search of them. On the way back she looked from side to side between the trees. Then she stopped right under the apple tree. 'What's this?' she asked, picking up something from the grass. 'Since when did strawberry hulls fall from apple trees?' Without even looking up she said in a half-cross, half-amused voice, 'Would the young ladies who are sitting on the branches above my head please descend to ground level?'

Katherine and her friends started to scramble down the tree, remembering just in time to untuck their dresses from their belts. Sister Mary would not have been pleased to see their underwear!

'Young ladies,' the nun said, 'each one of you comes from a good home and your parents have placed you here to be cared for. At the end of your convent schooling they expect to take home young ladies, not squirrels that steal fruit and scramble up trees. What would your mothers say? You'll do extra Latin homework this afternoon. And, to pay for the strawberries, you can help me in the garden for an hour tomorrow afternoon.' The nun strode off leaving seven cross children behind her. But Katherine could never stay cross for long. 'Catch me if you can!' she called, as she ran in the opposite direction.

That afternoon Sister Mary took Katherine aside. 'I'm disappointed in you,' she told her. 'How long were you in your last convent?'

'I think I went when I was three,' the child answered.

'And seven years later you've not learned to behave!' the nun accused. 'Well, you'll soon learn. Marienthron is the best convent in Germany. And the sooner you learn the better. You're a bad influence on the other girls.' Katherine did learn to behave herself, at least when the nuns were looking!

'I've decided to become a nun,' she told one of her friends, when she was sixteen years old. 'I've grown to like this place and I do want to please God. In any case, I've lived in a convent since before I can remember and I wouldn't know how to live anywhere else.'

'We've also decided to be nuns,' two of her friends said. They were sisters. A little group of girls took their vows together, promising not to marry, not to have belongings of their own, and to stay in the convent for the rest of their lives.

'I need to talk to you,' Katherine said to her friend one day the following year. 'Meet me under the apple tree. And tell the others too.' After the day's work was done the friends met together under the tree.

'What is it?' one of them asked.

'Listen,' Katherine von Bora said. 'Wait till I tell you this. A monk was visiting near here. His name's Martin Luther. Apparently he preached in German and not in Latin!'

'Wow!' said one of the young nuns. 'He'll be in trouble for that!'

'And he said that if we had faith in God we would go to heaven, not if we did good works!'

'You're kidding!' another of the girls gasped. 'But wouldn't that be wonderful?'

'And,' went on Katherine, 'he said that we can pray to God instead of praying to the saints.'

'What are you doing?' Sister Mary asked. Nobody had seen her coming.

'Just talking,' Katherine explained. Somehow she knew that Sister Mary would not agree with the monk and that she'd better watch her step. But that didn't stop the young woman thinking.

Gossip came and went from the convent

by the carriers who brought in supplies and who took the nuns' fruit, vegetables and honey to the nearby market.

'Luther says we don't need to be in a convent to serve God.' 'Luther says that the Pope isn't head of the church.' 'Luther says there's no such place as purgatory!'

That set the young women thinking. 'Does he mean that Christians go to heaven when they die rather than purgatory?'

'It must,' Katherine agreed. 'And he says that all his ideas come from the Bible!'

'Guess what else he says?' one of her friends giggled. The group waited to hear what was coming. 'He says that priests can get married!'

Every few days there seemed to be more news of the monk, Martin Luther. And each time the news made the girls think about what they really believed.

Twelve young nuns, including Katherine von Bora, decided they would have to leave the convent.

'There's no way we can stay here when our hearts are telling us to get out and to follow the truth of the Bible rather than what the Roman Church is teaching.'

'It's exciting!' one of her friends said.

Her sister shivered. 'It's terrifying.'

'I think we should write to Martin Luther for advice,' the most sensible suggested. And his reply was to send a local merchant to help them escape. On 7th April 1523 a student ran into Luther's town of Wittenberg and told his friends, 'A wagon-load of young women have just come to town, all more excited at the thought of being married than they are about being alive!'

Indeed, the girls did marry one after the other until only Katherine was left. 'I think you should marry her,' Luther's friend told him. 'She'd make a very good wife for you.'

'You say priests can marry,' another said, 'then why not monks? And you could lead the way.'

'I want you to marry,' Martin's father said. 'And when you have a son he will carry the name Luther to another generation.'

It took him some time to make up his mind, but Martin did discuss marriage with Katherine.

'I believe that there is a great change, a reformation going on in Europe,' he said. 'The Roman Church has taught errors for so long that we now need to preach the Bible loud and clear, and we need to have it in our own language too. You know that I've made enemies by saying these things in public?' he asked.

'Yes,' replied the young woman.

'And do you realise that some people have been burned at the stake for preaching what

I preach?'

'Yes,' she said.

'And you're still prepared to marry me?'

'Yes,' was her firm reply, 'I am.'

On 13th June 1525 Katherine von Bora became Mrs Katherine Luther and she went to live in the monastery with her new husband.

Before long Katherine made sure her husband was interested in more than church problems. He became a keen gardener and they had hens, ducks, pigs and cows. Working in the garden and orchard helped him to relax.

'Martin needed a wife,' Katherine thought, 'and I'm so glad it's me.' And he did need a wife. Luther was so generous that he sometimes gave away things they needed. Once when he was about to do that his wife found out. 'I'm sending you a vase,' he wrote to someone in need, and then added, 'Katie's hidden it.' A year after they were married Martin had good news to tell. 'My dear Katie presented me with a little Hans Luther yesterday at two o'clock, by God's grace.'

'Our first year of marriage was so happy,' Katie told a friend, 'but this year is hard going. The plague has hit several times and little Hans has been terribly ill.

Though Martin has not had the plague he is suffering from depression. When he's very down I read the Bible to him or get one of his friends to keep him company. Music seems to help him too.' By the end of the year Hans had a little sister called Elizabeth who would help cheer up their daddy. But little Elizabeth only lived for eight months.

'Katie, I'm needing your help today,' Martin often said. 'When I'm translating the Bible into German I want to use the words that ordinary people would use. You're so good with words, will you come and help me?' 'Yes,' Katie would reply. 'I'll come.'

'What's the common word for making bread rise?' he asked. 'Not the long word that cooks use, the word that ordinary housewives would say.' His wife gave him the word he was looking for.

'What are you translating today?' she asked.

'It's Jesus' story about a little yeast making a whole loaf rise just as a little sin makes a whole life bad.'

'Well, I think that's the word you want.'

'The more I preach the Bible the more enemies I have,' Martin said to his wife one day. 'But there needs to be change in the church. Are you remembering this might cost me my life and you your husband?'

'God will care for us,' Katie said. 'Don't be frightened for us.' Her attitude allowed Luther to preach freely and to risk even his life for the truth of the Bible.

But life in the Luther household was not always so serious. Martin could be great fun. He even had a bowling alley built in the monastery!

'How many children do you have now?' a visitor asked Katie, when their last one was born. 'We have six of our own,' she said, 'as well as eleven orphans. Some students of Martin's stay with us too.'

'My darling Katie keeps me young,' Martin told the visitor, 'and fit too,' he laughed. 'Without her I'd be totally lost. She puts up with my travels and she's always waiting for me when I come back. She nurses me through my depressions. She's patient with my tantrums. She helps with my work. And most of all she loves Jesus. Apart from God's gift of his Son, she's the best gift he has given me in all of my life.'

Katie squeezed his hand.

'All I've been is a wife and mother,' Katie commented, when they were alone. 'And I think I must have been one of the happiest wives and mothers in all of Germany.'

Katherine Luther

Martin held her close. 'Darling Katie,' he said, stroking her hair, 'I believe God has used me to help change the church for all time. And I couldn't have done it without you. If the history of this Reformation is ever written I hope and pray that your name will be there with mine in the history books.' And it is.

Fact File: Latin. This was the original language of the Roman Empire and until about the 9th century Latin was the only written language in Western Europe. Latin survived long after the collapse of the Roman Empire and was used throughout Western Europe by merchants, scholars and churchmen. Reformers such as Wycliffe and Luther however wanted the Bible to be read by everyone and not just educated people, and that's why they pushed to have the Bible translated into languages other than Latin.

 Keynote: Katherine and her friends were delighted to hear that purgatory did not exist and that the Bible had nothing to say about it at all. One of the great things about following Jesus Christ and trusting in him is that when you die you will immediately go to be with him in heaven.

Think: Katherine did not write books or preach sermons but she was an invaluable help to Luther who did do these things. She was a great support to him. She looked after him and gave him advice. Katherine was hard working and clever and God used her abilities to bring his Word to the ordinary people. Ask God to use you to bring his Word to other people who do not know him yet.

Prayer: Thank you God for giving us your Word, the Bible. Thank you that I can read it in my own language. Thank you for schools and books that have taught me to read. Please help missionaries round the world who are translating your Word into other languages. When I read your Word help me to understand it and obey it. Help me to tell it to others. Amen.

Susanna Wesley

Susanna counted, '… seventeen, eighteen, nineteen, twenty.'

'Well done!' her mother said. 'You're a clever girl. Now, what comes after twenty?'

The child thought. 'Twenty-one?' she asked.

'That's right. And then what?' But Susanna had reached the end of her numbers. 'Let's sing the number song to her,' Mrs Annesley told some of her other children.

'One, two, three … Twenty-one, twenty-two, twenty-three,' they sang to the tune of a nursery rhyme, 'twenty-four and twenty-five's Susanna.'

Then they all fell about in a fit of giggles. The youngest of them laughed too though she didn't know what they were all laughing about.

'Why do you always sing "twenty-five's Susanna?" the five-year-old asked one of her brothers.

He grinned. 'It's because Dad and Mum had twenty-five children and you're the youngest. That makes you the twenty-fifth!'

Susanna held up both hands and looked at all ten fingers. Then she made her hands into fists and opened them up again. 'That's twenty,' she told her brother. She made one fist and opened that hand again. 'And that comes to twenty-five. That's a lot of children,' the girl said. She made her little finger dance. 'And this one is twenty-five's Susanna!'

'I think we should be getting on with your school work,' Mrs Annesley told her youngest children. Three sat down on the floor at her knee to continue the lesson on counting. Four were on chairs round the table where they had reading to do. And four others were in Dr Annesley's study learning history with him. The rest were either out at work or away from home. When it was nearly lunch-time their father came into the living-room to ask them their daily questions. From a little book of questions and answers, which he called a catechism, he asked each a question.

'Who made you?' he smiled at Susanna.

'God made me,' she replied. Then it was the turn of the next one up.

'Why did God make you?'

'God made me to worship and adore him.'
'What else did God make?'
'God made all things.'

By the time Dr Annesley reached the oldest child the questions were really quite difficult. But as he asked them every day they all knew the answers.

'Where's Susanna? We want her to come out and play with us,' the little girl heard one of her sisters asking. But Susanna didn't answer. She was under the table in her father's study where he and his friends couldn't see her because of the heavy tablecloth that reached right down to the floor.

Although she didn't understand most of what the men talked about she still loved to hear them speaking. Susanna pictured their faces. When her father said the name of Jesus she knew his face would look warm and soft. And when sin was being discussed she imagined his expression being sad. Whenever heaven was mentioned she knew exactly how he would look, for her father couldn't speak about heaven without his eyes smiling. But the talk went on for a long, long time and the child fell asleep.

'I think your pet is under the table again,' one of the visitors commented. A man who was new to the group thought there must be a dog in the room. But Dr Annesley knew better. He took a cushion from behind him and held it out to his friend. 'Put that under her head please,' he said.

'I'd like to have a talk with you, Dad,' Susanna said, seven or eight years later.

'Come into my study,' her father smiled. 'There's nowhere else to talk quietly in this busy house.'

'Now, what's worrying you?' he asked, when they were settled by the wood fire.

Susanna knew this could be difficult, but she had thought out what she wanted to say. 'I understand you felt strongly that you shouldn't join the Church of England when Parliament said all ministers had to. That's why you weren't able to preach in public until King Charles said you could do again. But I really believe that I should belong to the Church of England.'

Dr Annesley looked at his daughter. 'I've brought this on myself,' he thought. 'I've taught them all to use their brains and to think for themselves.'

'Tell me why you think so,' he asked Susanna.

The girl gave very clear reasons why she should leave the Dissenters and join the Church of England. And that's what she did shortly afterwards.

'Who's that young man?' Susanna asked her sister one day.

'That's Samuel Wesley, and you and he have something in common.' The girl looked at the stranger and wondered what that might be. 'We're about the same height,' she teased. 'Only he's stopped growing and I'll get taller than I am just now.'

Her sister laughed. 'It's not only your height you have in common, you're as strong-minded as each other.'

'How do you know that?' asked Susanna.

'Because he did exactly the same as you did. He left the Dissenters and went back to the Church of England.'

'Interesting...' thought the young Susanna. 'We do have something in common after all.'

'November 1688,' wrote the nineteen-year-old bride in her diary, 'I married Samuel Wesley, minister of the Church of England. We're starting married life in London where I'm going to have to be the best housewife in the whole city to make £28 a year feed and clothe us.'

'I need two new shirts,' Samuel told Susanna, some months after they were married.

'I'm afraid you'll have to wait,' she explained. 'There's hardly enough money for food let alone new shirts. But I'll patch your old ones very carefully.'

Samuel held up an ancient shirt. 'You'll just be joining patches together,' he grumped. 'If you can't manage on what I earn here I'll just have to find another job.'

Susanna wondered what expense she could cut back on, but she couldn't think of a single thing.

'I can have my new shirts now!' Wesley announced, as be burst into their little home some months later. 'I'm going to be a minister to the crew of a boat that works back and forward across the Irish Sea.'

Susanna looked horrified, thinking that she might have to live on board! She heaved a sigh of relief when he went on, 'You can stay in a boarding house while I'm away. And we'll be able to afford that because I'll be earning £70 a year.' But after just six months Samuel was back on land and looking for yet another job. Being at sea didn't agree with him at all.

'You're a grandfather once again!' Mrs Annesley announced to her husband when, in 1690, little Samuel Wesley was born. She took her husband by the arm into the next-door bedroom where their daughter's baby had just been born. 'Hello Grandfather,'

Susanna said, as though the tiny infant in her arms was speaking. Samuel screwed up his eyes and looked at the world. He couldn't have thought much of it because he opened his mouth and yelled.

'I wonder if he'll be a preacher one day,' Dr Annesley said. 'He's certainly got the lungs for it.'

Susanna handed the baby to her mother and cuddled down to sleep, grateful that she had been able to come home for his birth. Her parents' home seemed so much more comfortable than any of the ones she and her husband had had in their first year and a half of marriage.

'Where's South Ormsby?' Susanna asked some months later, when Samuel told her they were moving there.

'It's in Lincolnshire,' he explained. 'It's a little village with a population of just over two hundred.'

'Lincolnshire!' wailed Susanna. 'That's worlds away from here.'

'Nonsense! It's only a hundred and fifty miles away. And you'll grow to like the countryside.'

Susanna picked up the baby even though he was sound asleep. She needed someone to cuddle while she did some serious thinking.

41

'That means I won't see my parents. And I won't see my brothers and sisters either. What about my friends? They're not able to travel as far as that and I can't afford to come back and see them.'

Tears started to roll down her face. She hugged baby Samuel close, wiping the tears away on his shawl so that her husband didn't see them.

'What's the house like?' she asked.

'It's simple,' her husband explained. 'Just a country house made of mud, with one room and a loft.'

Susanna thought of her parents' home. 'Do you know anything else about it?' she asked, dreading the answer.

'I understand that the village women are cleaning it out for us.'

She risked a smile. 'That's kind of them. Anything else?'

'Oh yes,' he said, turning away as he spoke, 'It seems that there's no glass in the windows but there are shutters so it should be cosy enough.'

'No glass!' thought Susanna. 'And no natural light when the shutters are closed!' She sat down, rocking the baby to comfort herself, when a thought struck her. 'If that's where God wants us to be then it's the best place for us.'

Susanna Wesley

The Wesleys spent seven years in South Ormsby before moving to Epworth where they had a bigger home for their growing family.

'Will you run a school for us in Epworth?' one of the children asked, as they packed up their slates and chalk for the last time in their old home.

'I certainly will,' Susanna told her. 'I started the school as soon as my first little boy was old enough to begin learning and I'll keep it going until the last of you girls is taught.'

'What's the most important lesson?' the girl asked.

'Is it reading or writing or counting?'

'They're all important,' her mother explained, 'but the most important lesson you can learn is that you need to trust in Jesus to be saved. There is nothing in the whole wide world more important than that.'

'Mrs Wesley has a little school in the rectory,' Samuel told some members of his new congregation. He was quite happy for more pupils to attend the classes his wife ran from nine to twelve each morning and from two till five in the afternoons. He was especially happy if some parents gave a small gift towards the school as he was forever running out of money.

'I hear Mr Wesley's wife is very strict,' the news went round the village after two of the local children joined the class.

'She is,' one of her new pupils admitted, when he was asked about his teacher. 'She's very, very strict. But she's fair with it.'

'Mrs Wesley's having Sunday meetings in the rectory,' was the local gossip one day. 'Her husband is away from home and although his assistant is taking services she thinks there should be afternoon meetings too,' one of Susanna's neighbours told her friend. 'Will you come to the meeting with me?'

'Yes, I'll come along,' her friend agreed. And they went.

'Did you see how well the Wesley children listened to the sermon their mother read to us?' the neighbour commented as the two women walked home afterwards.

'I did indeed,' was the reply. 'No wonder she teaches our Tommy so well!'

'You must use your brains,' Susanna told her children and other pupils over and over again. 'Think everything through for yourselves. And the most important thing to think through is this, where will you go when you die? You may decide not to believe in God when you're alive but do you think God will be taken in on the Judgment Day when you tell him he doesn't exist?' And when, in 1709, their home burned down, and their five-year-old son John was only just rescued from the flames, she reminded her family yet again that one day they would all have to meet their maker.

Samuel soon had a new house underway, and when they moved into it Susanna wrote her thoughts down in her diary. 'Another new home, and a nice solid one too. I'm glad it's built of brick. It's so much safer than wood,' she added, thinking back to the fire. 'I suppose it's because the new house gives us a new beginning that I'm thinking back over the years. They've not been easy but I have so much to thank God for. Of our nineteen babies, we have ten still alive, though poor Mary is crippled. Some of them are now Christians and that is the joy of my heart. I'll pray for the others to be converted until the day I die. And every day I pray that God will use my dear children to spread the good news that Jesus saves.'

As the years passed and the children moved away from home, Susanna wrote more in her diary, especially as her husband was difficult to live with. 'It seems that God is calling Charles and John to preach the gospel,' she wrote. 'My heart is singing!'

And they did become preachers, two of the most famous preachers England ever had. Like their mother they had minds of their own. And also like Susanna they left the church they'd been brought up in. But they didn't join another of the churches in England; they started the Methodist Church, which has since spread throughout England and to many other countries in the world.

Fact File: Brains. Sometimes we can be told to use our brains! This means to think something through. But here are some facts about brains you may not know. The brain of a grown-up weighs about 1.3 kilograms. It is made up of approximately 15,000,000,000 cells. Your body is controlled by three different parts of your brain. The cerebrum controls body movement. It helps you to think and learn as well as experience emotions. The cerebellum helps you to balance and it makes sure that your legs and arms work properly together. The medulla is very small and regulates your heart beat and breathing. The brain is a wonderful thing. It didn't happen by accident. God designed it!

Keynote: Susanna thought for herself. She made decisions for herself even when she was quite young. But more importantly she prayed about these decisions. It is important to think for yourself but it is more important to think about what God wants.

Our thoughts and decisions can be wrong if we are not asking God to help and guide us.

Think: Susanna said that wherever God sent them that would be the best place for them to be. Sometimes we have to move away to another town or city. It can be a difficult and exciting time. If you trust in God you will realise that he always wants what is best for you. Ask God to show you how to be useful to him wherever you are.

Prayer: Lord help me to obey you and trust you whatever happens in my life. You are always with me wherever I go. Help me to be obedient to your Word wherever I am. Amen

Ann Judson

Ann and her three sisters stood against the wall, each with a feather at her feet. 'Ready, steady, go!' their brother shouted from the other end of the room. All four girls scrambled down on to their hands and knees and began to blow their feathers along the floor.

'That's my one!' the oldest girl laughed, as she reached up to catch a feather that was in danger of blowing away.

'Come on!' their brother called. 'If you don't watch out Ann will win again.'

Three of the girls blew with big breaths and their feathers went everywhere. Ann, blowing with little breaths, kept her feather under control and in front of all the others. 'I've won!' she announced, when her feather hit the far wall of the room. 'Now, what's the next game?'

Mr and Mrs Hasseltine smiled from their seats by the fire. 'I just love to see them playing together,' Mrs Hasseltine said. 'I'd rather listen to the children's laughter than music.'

Her husband nodded. 'The new room will give them plenty of space to play just now and we can use it for parties and dances when they're older.'

'Shall we tell them about it?' Mrs Hasseltine asked.

'What a good idea,' he agreed.

'Your mother and I have something to tell you,' Mr Hasseltine said, when the next game was over. The children sat down in front of the fire. Usually when their father said that there was a treat in store. 'We've decided to build another room on to the house, a big room to use for parties. And when you're older we'll hold balls in it too.'

Young John screwed up his face.

'By then there will be four young ladies looking for handsome husbands,' Mrs Hasseltine said, looking at her four daughters. 'Where better to meet young men than at a ball in your very own home.'

'That sounds wonderful!' Ann said.

'Balls sound boring,' teased her brother.

'Please be ready to leave for church in fifteen minutes,' Mrs Hasseltine told the girls one Sunday morning.

'I'll never be ready on time,' thought Ann. 'I can't decide which dress to wear.' There were four spread out on her bed, all with matching underwear. Along the pillow was a selection of hats, each with a variety of ribbons to choose from. 'If I wore my yellow dress I could put on the hat with blue and yellow ribbons. Or if I wore my pink dress I could choose between that hat and this one. But then I couldn't take my new yellow fan. She sat down in a heap of satin underskirt to make up her mind.

'Five minutes!' her father's voice called. Ann grabbed the yellow dress and slipped it on. She wrapped each of her ringlets round her finger, letting them fall loosely on her shoulders. Picking up her new fan, she peeked from behind it to see how she looked in the mirror. 'I must run,' she said, holding up the hems of her long dress to prevent herself tripping.

'Well! Well!' laughed Mr Hasseltine, as she ran down the stair. 'If I don't have the loveliest daughters in America, I don't know who has ... and the handsomest son too.'

Ann loved Sundays. After church the family had a meal together then went for a walk in the afternoon sun. The evening was spent reading or singing round the piano. Never a day passed in the Hasseltine home without a great deal of laughter and fun, and Sundays were no different. That night as she went to bed, Ann wrote in her diary,

'I think I am one of the happiest creatures on earth.'

'Don't forget to say your prayers,' Mrs Hasseltine said every night at bedtime. 'Remember to ask God to forgive you for all you've done wrong today.'

As it was so warm that Ann couldn't sleep, she lay thinking about what her mother had said. 'I wish I could stop doing wrong things,' she decided. 'I really do try but I don't always manage.' Then she remembered a party she was invited to and, before she could stop herself, she was working out what she would wear.

'Our new teacher is very serious,' Ann's older sister said. 'I think Bradford Academy won't be nearly such fun now he's come.'

'He says that if we don't trust in Jesus and have our sins forgiven we'll go to hell when we die.'

Mr Hasseltine smiled at his children. 'This seems a very serious topic of conversation,' he commented, 'perhaps too serious for dinner-time.'

'But it would be very serious if we went to hell,' Ann said, 'so I'm going to try my very, very hardest to be good and go to heaven.'

Ann, who was by then fifteen years old, did try very hard. She read her Bible every day; she remembered to pray each morning and evening, and she tried to be much more serious.

'It's not enough just to try to be good,' her teacher told his class. 'You must repent and be forgiven.'

Ann listened to what he said and it troubled her. She listened hard at church and she went to other Christian meetings as well. But it wasn't at church, or at a meeting, that Ann Hasseltine became a Christian. It was through a loving Christian aunt who explained to her that she had to confess her sins and believe in Jesus to be saved. 'Now I really am one of the happiest people on earth,' she decided. 'My sins are forgiven. Jesus is my Saviour and friend, and I know that when I die I'll go home to heaven.'

'We're having a group of young people for lunch,' Mrs Hasseltine told the family. They were now grown-up and Ann was a teacher. 'Make them all feel very welcome.'

'Would you like more soup?' Ann asked one of the young men, when he had finished what was in his plate.

'No thank you,' he said, then changed his mind. 'It's worth a second plate of soup to have a closer look at Ann,' he thought. 'She's beautiful. Her skin is so smooth and her eyes sparkle. Her black curly hair is just perfect. Not only that, I can hear from what she says that she's a Christian!' There was no doubt about it, their visitor, Adoniram Judson, had a very serious case of falling in love!

Not many months passed before Adoniram made an appointment to speak to Mr Hasseltine.

'I love Ann,' he told the older man, 'and I should like to make her my wife.'

'What kind of life will she have if she marries you?' the girl's father asked.

Judson looked him straight in the eye. This was not going to be easy. 'I believe God is calling me to be a missionary in Burma. If Ann marries me she will have a life of service but it will be a hard and sometimes dangerous one. As a small group of us hope to travel together Ann would have company for the voyage. Beyond that I really don't know. But God does,' he added.

'This isn't a decision I feel I should take,' Mr Hasseltine said. 'I will leave it up to Ann.'

When she replied to Adoniram's proposal of marriage, Ann wrote, 'I dare not decline an offer I believe to be God's will even though many are ready to call it a wild romantic undertaking.' They were married in 1811.

The journey to Burma took a very long time as they had to stay for a while in India. By the time they arrived they had faced many dangers including a near shipwreck. They had said sad farewells to the other young missionaries who sailed from America with them. And, most terrible of all, Adoniram and Ann's first baby was born dead and buried at sea. It was a broken-hearted Ann Judson who arrived in Burma.

She wrote home soon after their arrival, 'This country is full of beauty and ugliness. The women are dressed in the brightest silks. They look like butterflies, and the rustle of silk sounds like butterfly wings. But when you look at their faces it's different. They chew something called betel that turns their mouths and teeth red; sometimes it even drips down their chins! The children often wear nothing at all apart from bits of string tied around their wrists, ankles and middles. These strings are meant to protect them from evil spirits! And believe it or not children as young as one smoke cigars! This is a very beautiful country, but such a strange one. What a difference it would make to the people if they were to believe in the Lord Jesus.'

'How will we ever learn to read this script?' Ann asked her husband, when they had settled down with a teacher. 'It looks just like a line of circles!'

Andoniram looked into Ann's lovely dark

eyes, 'We'll learn it,' he said, 'because we need to. There's no way of translating the Bible into Burmese without learning the language!'

Ann grinned. 'When you put it like that it makes perfect sense!' she said.

Both the Judsons were good at languages, and before very long they were able to read and write some Burmese.

'Things are becoming dangerous,' Judson told Ann, after they had been missionaries in Burma for twelve years. 'With England and Burma at war we're suspected of being spies. The Burmese can't tell the difference between the English and Americans.'

'It's not just us,' Ann said, looking at the two Burmese children in the room. 'We have these two little girls to look after now and whatever happens we must keep the translation safe. It would be a tragedy if all these years of work were lost.' Ann looked round their little home. It was made of bamboo and built on stilts like all the other homes around them. She sat down to think.

'Are you tired?' Adoniram asked, full of concern for his pregnant wife.

'I'm weary,' she admitted, 'and if I don't keep praying I feel fearful.'

Adoniram held her close. 'Maung Ing will

look after you if anything happens to me,' he told her, knowing that their Burmese servant would do everything in his power to help them.

The door flew open the following evening, just as the family was about to eat. 'You're called by the King,' an official screamed, as he scrambled up the bamboo ladder and into the room. Two ferocious men climbed in behind him. 'Spotted Faces!' the little girls screamed. Ann threw her long wide skirt around the children to prevent them seeing Adoniram being thrown to the floor before having his elbows tied behind his back. Maung Ing was horrified. The Spotted Faces were murderers and thugs the authorities used to do their dirty work. Ann pushed the girls in Maung Ing's direction and he hid them. 'Don't take my husband away!' she cried, but she could do nothing to stop him being thrown down the steps. Ann rushed to where she kept her money and raced after the men. They took what she paid them to slacken Adoniram's ropes, but they didn't do anything to make their prisoner more comfortable.

'Help me! Maung Ing,' Ann begged, as she climbed up the bamboo ladder. 'They'll be back to search the place.' She grabbed the New Testament translation. 'Get any old cloth you can find,' she urged. He scrabbled round and brought what she was looking for. 'Get string!' she told the wide-eyed girls. 'Find me string!' Kneeling on the floor Maung Ing and Ann wrapped up the translation work and tied it tight. 'Wait here,' she said to the two little girls. 'You can watch from the door.' Turning to Maung Ing she said, 'We've got to bury this! We've got to keep it away from the Spotted Faces.' Ann and Maung Ing dug a hole near the house and buried the precious bundle. Then he stamped the earth to look like everywhere else. The pair of them climbed back up to the girls. 'We're just on time,' whispered Maung Ing. 'They're coming back!'

'Adoniram's in Death Prison,' was the news that Ann dreaded. It was an unspeakable place where prisoners were hung up by their feet every night with only their necks and heads on the ground. Ann visited her husband, and watched him getting filthier and weaker and eventually unable to walk.

'Take this pillow to Adoniram,' she told Maung Ing two months later. The prisoner's eyes lit up. It was the bumpiest and most uncomfortable pillow ever, but Adoniram hugged it close. He had his precious translation work back in his arms!

'Tell Ann I love her and thank God for her,' he said, to his faithful servant.

In all the terrible things that happened during that war, God kept the translation work safe. Adoniram and Ann's baby daughter Maria was born while he was still in prison. On the very last day of 1825 he was released from prison, having been held in desperate conditions for a year and a half.

However, by the end of the following year both Ann and Maria had died. Some time later Adoniram married again and continued with the work he and Ann had begun and the Burmese people got God's Word in their own language.

But if it had not been for Ann Judson's quick thinking the Burmese translation of the Bible might not have happened at all.

Fact File: Burma. The country of Burma is now known as Myanmar. You will find it on an atlas at the eastern side of the Bay of Bengal. It is surrounded by the countries of Bangladesh, India, China, Laos and Thailand. Over half of Myanmar is forest and the city of Rangoon is situated on the coast. Rangoon has 24.5 metres of rain each year. However some mountainous regions of Myanmar have over 50 metres of rain every year.

Keynote: Ann thought that the country of Burma was very beautiful but there were other things that frightened and disturbed her about it. However, Ann recognised that what the Burmese people needed was to believe in the Lord Jesus Christ. That is what you need - that is what your country needs wherever you live.

Ann Judson

Think: Ann wanted to go to heaven as she knew that hell was a real and awful place. She did not want to go there. However, she thought that in order to get to heaven she would have to earn salvation. Anne thought she had to become good before she would be allowed to go. But Jesus tells us that the only way to heaven and to God is through him. It is by believing and trusting in Jesus Christ that we are given eternal life. It is only Jesus who can make us ready for heaven.

Prayer: Lord Jesus, show me how sinful I am and show me how wonderful you are. Make me ready to go to heaven to be with you. Amen

Maria Taylor

Maria and Burella Dyer looked at each other, each wondering how her sister felt about what their step-father had just told them.

'I've thought a lot about your future. I've prayed about it too,' he went on. 'And I really don't see any alternative to sending you both back to England. Your uncle and aunt have agreed to care for you.'

'But China is our home,' Maria said. 'We belong here.'

'We're almost Chinese,' added Burella. 'We won't know anyone at school in England. We'll always be the odd ones out.'

The kind man smiled at his step-daughters. 'You will fit in after a while,' he assured them. 'But I have to confess that life in China won't be the same without you.'

Maria saw her chance. 'Then let us stay,' she pleaded.

He shook his head. 'I'm truly sorry. But that's just not possible.'

'Happy birthday to you!' Burella sang to her sister on 16th January 1847. 'Imagine you being ten years old!'

Maria rubbed her sleepy eyes. 'It's not a happy birthday,' she moaned. 'It's the saddest birthday in my whole life because it's the last one I'll have in China. In less than a month we sail for England.'

Burella, who was eleven, hugged her sister tight. 'I know it is,' she said. 'But I have a plan.'

'What's that?' asked Maria.

Burella replied, 'When we go to England we'll study very hard and become teachers. Then we can come back to China and be missionaries ourselves. Nobody could send us back to England then.'

The birthday girl cheered up. 'And we could run our own school,' she laughed. 'You could be the headmistress and I could be the infant teacher.'

'Don't let's tell anyone,' Burella warned. 'Let's keep it a secret.'

'Goodbye!' the little group of missionaries yelled, 'Goodbye!' The Dyer girls waved from the boat as it eased away from the quay. They waved and waved, tears streaming down their faces so that they could hardly see their friends who had come to see them off.

Suddenly the group on shore burst into song, 'God bless you and keep you, God care for you dear friends. God bless you and keep you now and till Jesus comes again.'

Burella wiped away her tears. 'They think we won't meet again until we're in heaven,' she told her little sister. 'But we'll be back one day. Dry your eyes,' she ordered. 'Or you'll miss your last sight of China.'

Maria did what she was told and as the land faded into the distance she imagined that ten years had passed, and that she and her sister were on their way back, catching their first sight of China, not their last.

'Why are you being sent back to England?' a boy travelling on the same boat asked.

'Our parents came from England,' Maria explained. 'They were missionaries in China. But Dad died when I was five. Two years after that Mum married again. Our step-father is also a missionary.'

'Was he kind to you?' the boy asked.

'Oh yes,' said Maria. 'He's very kind.'

'So why is he sending you away?'

The girl took up her story again. 'A year after Mum married again she became ill and died, leaving our step-father to take care of us.'

The boy looked shocked. 'So you've not got a real dad or mum of your own now?' he asked.

'No,' Maria agreed. 'But we've still got our step-father even though he can't care for us.'

'Who will look after you?'

'We're going back to England to stay with our uncle and aunt.'

'Are they nice?' she was asked.

'I think so,' the girl said. Her new friend was full of questions.

'Have you met them before?' was the next one.

Maria said she had, 'but I don't remember them very well. We lived in England from when I was two till I was four, but that was a long time ago.'

'I remember lots of things from when I was four!' the boy announced.

For the next five years the Dyer sisters worked hard, first at school then at a college where they trained as teachers.

'Every day is a day nearer China,' Burella often said to her sister. And Maria would smile at the thought, though China sometimes seemed a long time ago and a very long way away.

'Do you think we will go back one day?' she asked.

'I don't think there's been a single day since we came home when I've not thought about going back,' her sister told her. 'All that's to be worked out is when and how.'

'There's a letter for you, Burella,' a teacher at the college said to her one day when she was sixteen years old.

The girl tore it open, 'It's from Mum's friend Miss Aldersey!' she told Maria. 'Listen to this.

"Your uncle tells me that you've done well in your teacher training and that you would now be able to take a class. I am writing to ask you to come back to China, to teach at my school at Ningpo. You would be teaching Chinese girls. While some of your pupils will be your own age or older, from what your uncle says I think you could cope with that."'

Maria's face fell. She had a sudden vision of losing her sister, of being left in England alone.

Burella read on. '"And if you bring Maria with you she, too, could help in the school!"' Their eyes met, sparkling with a mixture of excitement and tears.

'We're going back to China!' the older girl laughed and cried. 'We're going home!'

That night Maria lay in bed thinking. 'I can hardly believe it,' she smiled. 'In just a few months we'll be in China, not as daughters of missionaries but as teachers ourselves. Dad and Mum would have been pleased to think we were missionaries.' Then she thought for a minute. 'I suppose what would have pleased them even more is that we're both Christians. That's what's most important of all. I remember when I was a little girl telling Mum that I wanted to be a princess and she said it was more important to be a Christian. But then she said that when I was converted I'd become a daughter of the God who is King of Kings and I'd be a princess in the kingdom of heaven.' Maria went to sleep happy. In the next room Burella was trying to remember all she could about Miss Aldersey. But all that came into her mind was that she was very strict.

In 1852 Maria and Burella Dyer sailed for China as teachers. The school at Ningpo was for Chinese girls. And Burella's memory of Miss Aldersey was quite right. She was a good teacher and a good headmistress but she was strict, very strict.

'She's trying to be a mother to us,' Maria told her sister when the headmistress seemed to be running their lives.

'I know that,' Burella tried to smile. 'But she forgets that we grew up in England, and that we're not little girls any longer.'

Three years after their arrival at Ningpo there was an air of disapproval about the place.

'How dare an Englishman behave like that!'

argued Miss Aldersey. 'He has no idea how to behave. The Chinese treat him like one of themselves! And he even has the cheek to treat people's diseases when he's not a fully qualified doctor!'

'He's certainly different,' Burella said to her sister after they first met Hudson Taylor.

Maria smiled, thinking of the missionary they'd met. 'I think he suits his black pigtail,' she announced. 'And I think it's really quite brave of him to have his head shaved and grow a pigtail. Once he'd done that he couldn't really go on wearing western clothes, could he?'

Her sister thought about it. 'I suppose not,' she said. 'A pigtail and black suit and tie would look ridiculous.'

Maria went on, 'It may be that one day we'll have to dress like the Chinese and become real friends with them so that we can tell them about Jesus.' She caught a look on Burella's face. 'What are you grinning at?'

The older sister broke into a wide smile. 'I was trying to imagine Miss Aldersey in Chinese clothes!'

What happened after that was hard for both Maria and Hudson Taylor. They fell deeply in love but Miss Aldersey disapproved of Hudson so very much that she refused to let them see each other. When that didn't put a stop to their love the headmistress wrote to Maria's uncle telling him what an awful fellow Hudson was and saying that there was no way the two young people should be allowed to marry. It took many months for that letter to reach England and for a reply to arrive. But when it came back it was not as disapproving as Miss Aldersey hoped it would be. In any case, Maria was just coming up to her twenty-first birthday when she would be able to make up her mind for herself whom she would marry. There was never any doubt who that would be. She married the Englishman who dressed as though he was Chinese and became Mrs Hudson Taylor on 20th January 1858, two days after her twenty-first birthday.

Although Hudson and Maria loved each other, the beginning of married life was not altogether happy because the following year they lost their first baby, and just months later Burella became ill with cholera and died. She was just twenty-three years old. But in 1859 the young couple had a healthy little daughter whom they called Grace.

'There's so much work to do I hardly see you,' Hudson whispered into Grace's little ear. 'But that doesn't stop me loving you.' The baby cooed contently, and reached out for her daddy's pigtail. 'And if it wasn't for friends back home in England sending gifts of money there would be nothing to feed you on,' he thought aloud, as he stroked her neck.

'But God has never seen us hungry,' her husband said. Maria agreed, though both knew that there had been times when there was nothing at all in the cupboard and no money, yet food had always come from somewhere before hunger set in.

'Hudson, you're losing weight and you've no colour in your cheeks at all,' Maria said. 'If we don't go back to England for a while you're not going to survive.'

Her husband started to say that there was too much work to do for him to leave.

'Listen to me,' Maria said gently but firmly. 'Of the two hundred couples that came out here in 1807, forty men died and fifty-one women. We don't want that to be repeated in our generation too.'

Hudson knew she was right. 'I'll make arrangements for the ship,' he agreed. 'We'll take Grace home to meet the English side of her family and I can train as a doctor while we're there.'

The Taylors' trip home marked a new beginning. 'We can't depend on the CMS,' they said to each other from time to time.

'But we can depend on the Lord.'

One day Hudson put that into practice. He opened a bank account in the name of the China Inland Mission and paid in £10. He and Maria prayed and planned.

'We'll ask God for men and women to be missionaries in the parts of China where nobody has ever heard about Jesus,' Hudson said. 'And we'll not ask anyone for money,' he continued. 'When we have needs we'll pray for them to be met. Our missionaries will all do the same, working for no payment except from God.'

Maria's eyes shone. 'God has always cared for us and he'll do the same for the China Inland Missionaries,' she added.

When they returned to China in 1886, the Taylors, now with two sons, Herbert and Frederick, as well as Grace, took sixteen new missionaries with them. It was the beginning of the China Inland Mission.

Because she had been brought up in that country, Maria understood as nobody else could what was involved in the work. She and her husband made up rules for the missionaries which would seem very strict now, but they set the China Inland Mission up in such a way that it's still running today, though it's now called Overseas Missionary Fellowship (OMF). Through its work countless people have come to know Jesus.

It was 22nd August, 1870, and Hudson thought that his wife was dying. 'The Mission will go on long after us,' she told him. 'The people of China need it.' Hudson held her hand to his lips. 'Yes, it will,' he said, 'and you'll be remembered as the mother of the mission for all the love and wisdom and experience you've put into it.'

'It's not been easy,' Maria said weakly. Hudson thought of their children who had died, including Grace, and of the ones who were left who were now losing their mother.

'No,' he said, 'it's not been easy. But God has given us everything we've needed.'

By the next day it was clear that Maria would not live for more than a few hours. She and Hudson had a precious time together sharing and talking about the children and about her going home to heaven. By the time evening came, that's where she was.

Fact File: China. China covers an area of 9, 560, 990 square kilometres. It has a population of 1,273,111,300. It has two seasons - the wet summer and the dry winter. In South China you can find tigers, monkeys and salamanders. In the south west you also find rare animals such as the panda. The Chinese people speak several different languages but all their written script is the same.

Keynote: Maria realised that God was telling her to work for him in China. But she also realised that before you became a missionary you had to be a Christian. You can't work for God if you haven't asked him to forgive your sins.

Think: Maria's life was not easy. She was ill, her children fell ill and some of them died. She must have felt very sad at times. Think about what Maria suffered. She went through this because she realised the importance of telling the Chinese people about the Lord Jesus Christ. Jesus suffered too. He suffered more than anyone ever has or ever will when he died for our sins on the cross. He did this because of God's love for us. Christ's death was the only way to ensure that those who followed him could have eternal life in heaven when they died.

Prayer: Lord Jesus, thank you for suffering so that I can have eternal life. Make me a worker for you in my home, at my school, with my friends. Help me to tell those I know the truth about you. Amen.

Susannah Spurgeon

Susannah sat in church between her parents and watched the pulpit, trying not even to blink.

'I'm going to see the minister coming in the door today,' she told herself, as she struggled to prevent herself blinking. Her eyes felt dry. 'Come quickly!' she whispered. Her eyelids quivered. 'Quickly!!' Then she blinked despite herself. And in the second her eyes were closed the minister went into the pulpit. 'Now I've got to wait another week to see it,' she thought crossly.

There were no steps up to the pulpit in her church and the minister came in through a door at the back. Every Sunday Susannah tried to see him open the door, come in and close it again ... and nearly every Sunday she blinked. 'I wonder if he really does come in the door or if he just appears there,' she puzzled.

Turning her eyes from the preacher, Susannah looked at the man who led the singing. 'I think he looks like a gigantic robin!' she decided, as she took in his unusual appearance. 'I know the clothes he wears are right for an old-fashioned lawyer, but they do look odd. I wonder why old-fashioned lawyers wore black long-tailed coats, knee breeches and silk stockings?' The girl found herself smiling. 'And he looks especially like a robin because he has such a round tummy!' She started to giggle softly.

'Are you all right?' Mrs Thompson asked.

'Yes, Mum,' her daughter answered, and tried to concentrate on the beginning of the service.

When she was a young teenager, Susannah became a Christian, but as the years passed she lost her enthusiasm. Although she still went to church and often enjoyed it, services didn't mean the same to her as they had done when she was first converted.

'I don't think I'll go to the service,' she decided one day. 'What I hear of the young man who is preaching doesn't appeal to me at all. He sounds very rough and ready.'

'Please come,' her friends said that afternoon.

'All right,' she agreed eventually. 'I'll go this evening just to please you.'

The church was full long before the

service and everyone watched for the little door in the back of the pulpit to open. Susannah didn't blink as it opened and she couldn't believe her eyes at what came in. Instead of a formal gentleman dressed in tailor-made clothes the preacher was a very young man whose suit looked as though a village dressmaker had made it! Not only that, he had a big black satin collar and he carried a blue handkerchief covered in white spots! She had never in her life seen anything like it, and she wasn't very pleased at all. That was Sunday 18th December 1853, a date Susannah wouldn't forget because the young man with the spotty handkerchief became her husband, Charles Spurgeon.

'Mr Spurgeon gave me a gift of Pilgrim's Progress by John Bunyan,' Susannah wrote in her diary some time later. 'And it has helped me such a lot. Although I've been a Christian for years I seemed to lose my love for the Lord. Thank goodness God never loses his love for his people. I feel as though I've fallen in love with Jesus all over again. Mr Spurgeon knew just the right book to give me. I can't imagine why I didn't like him when he first came to preach. I can understand why so many hundreds of people come to hear him.'

'It's 8th January 1856,' Susannah said to

herself as she wakened that morning. 'And it's our wedding day!' She spent most of the morning praying before dressing to be married.

'What's wrong?' she asked her father, as their carriage neared the church in central London. 'What are all these crowds waiting for?'

'I think they want to see you both arriving at the church and leaving,' Mr Thompson suggested.

His daughter was horrified. 'But there are thousands of them! Look! There are even police out to keep them off the road!' Susannah looked up a side street as they passed. 'The traffic has all stopped!' she said, unable to take in that she was the cause of the hold-up.

Her father smiled. 'And it will all be on the move again when you and your popular young man are married.'

Charles Haddon Spurgeon was Susannah's favourite preacher by far, and he was London's favourite preacher too. But one group of people didn't seem to like him at all. They were the newspaper reporters. It wasn't long after the young couple were married that Susannah began to collect newspaper cuttings in a scrapbook. Some reported things accurately but others told awful lies about her husband.

'Do the papers worry you?' Susannah asked him, after one particularly nasty article.

Charles smiled. 'When I look at my darling wifey I'm so happy that nothing worries me at all.'

And when twin boys were born nothing the papers could have said would have taken away Charles' joy! He was over the moon!

'Susannah seems to be taking a long time to recover from the twins' birth,' Charles commented to a doctor friend.

'She's probably just tired,' the doctor said. 'One baby's tiring enough, two is plain exhausting!'

Months later Spurgeon spoke to his friend again, but the reply was not as reassuring. 'You're right,' he said. 'Susannah is not looking well and she seems to have no energy at all. Let's hope it will pass.' But it never did.

Although Susannah had times when she was a little better she also had times when she couldn't get out of her bed for weeks.

'It makes me sad to see her so poorly,' Charles thought. 'Yet she hardly ever complains.'

'Is there anything I can get for you?'

Spurgeon asked one day when Susannah was really quite ill.

She thought for a moment then grinned. 'You could get me an opal ring and a bullfinch that will sing to me.'

Her husband smiled back, unsure if she was joking and knowing that he certainly couldn't afford an opal ring.

'This is for you,' Charles said, a short time afterwards. Susannah opened the little box and saw an opal ring. 'An old lady sent it to you as a present,' he explained.

A few months later Charles brought another gift for his sick wife – a bullfinch that would sing to her. She laughed at the little bird as it puffed out its chest and twittered. Maybe the man who led the singing in church when she was a girl had been more like a bullfinch than a robin!

In 1875 Charles handed his wife a book. 'It's the proof copy of my first book Lectures to my Students,' he explained. 'I've got to give it one last check then it goes for printing.'

Susannah looked at the book. 'I just wish every minister in England could have a copy,' she said.

Spurgeon looked serious. 'How much will you give to make that happen?' he asked. It was his wife's turn to look serious. Did he really mean what he'd said? Suddenly Susannah remembered some money she had saved and kept in an upstairs drawer. When she added that to what was in her bank account she discovered that she had enough to buy a hundred copies of the book. That was the beginning of Mrs Spurgeon's Book Fund.

'Ministers earning less than £150 a year are invited to apply to Mrs Spurgeon for a copy of her husband's book,' their church magazine said the following month.

'Listen to this!' Susannah exclaimed to her husband when she opened her mail one day. 'This poor minister gets only £60 a year and he hasn't bought a book for ten years!' 'Listen to this!' she said another day. 'The man who wrote this letter hasn't been able to buy his children winter coats let alone buy himself books.' 'Listen to ....' she began, when the next day's mail came.

'You're going to read me another sad letter,' Charles said, 'but don't let all the sadness get you down because what you're doing is making these poor folk happy.'

'I just can't take in what's happening,' Susannah told her husband, who had come to sit on her bed and talk to her. 'We're getting gifts of money sent to the Book Fund that almost exactly equal the letters applying for books. Today a gift of £25 came and letters came asking for £25 worth of books. Isn't God good!'

Charles nodded then looked around the room. 'What on earth are they?' he asked, pointing to a pile of tatty books in a corner.

His wife shook her head wearily. 'Unfortunately, people also send us books they seem to think might be useful.'

Spurgeon rose from the bed and picked up the top few books. 'Advice to Mothers! Letters to a Son! Butterflies of Britain!' he laughed. 'Are these meant to help poor preachers write their sermons?'

Susannah, who was by then desperately tired, shook her head. 'I'm afraid some people think that anything in the shape of a book should be sent to your tired wifey.'

Charles looked down at her pale face and his heart ached. He kissed her goodnight and she was asleep before he put the useless books back on the pile.

'You're as busy as someone with a full-time job,' Charles told his wife some years later. 'And you manage it all from your couch.'

'If I couldn't manage it from here I couldn't do it at all,' Susannah replied.

Spurgeon shook his head. 'How I wish you could be up and about. I wish you could get out to see the cherry blossom.'

'I can enjoy the memory of cherry blossom,' she said. 'And before you get any sadder I want you to sit down and hear some good news.'

Charles drew up a chair beside his wife and waited. If Susannah said she had good news it was worth paying close attention.

'Today a friend brought £100 for the Book Fund,' she began. 'I was so pleased because a lot of applications have arrived in the last few days. Then in the second post a bill came in for books I've bought in the last three months. I'd forgotten the bill was due. If the £100 had not come today the Book Fund would have been £60 in debt!'

'God knew what you needed even though you'd forgotten,' Charles said. 'How like him.'

'I know there are so many things I can't do,' Susannah said, taking her husband's hand, 'but he's so good in blessing the few things I can do.'

Spurgeon nodded. 'There are hundreds of ministers who would agree with you there.'

'How many books have you sent out altogether?' a visitor asked Susannah in 1888.

She picked up a huge notebook that was always beside her and opened it. 'In 1881,' she said, 'we distributed 7,298 books and 10,517 printed sermons that Charles had preached. Last year, that's seven years later, we distributed 10,311 books and 21,227 sermons.'

The visitor whistled. 'I suppose they go all over England,' he commented.

Mrs Spurgeon smiled. 'They do indeed, and to Africa, the West Indies and other countries as well.'

'How do you know where to send them?' the young man asked.

'Ministers write asking for books.'

Her visitor grinned. 'You must get a lot of letters!'

Susannah turned the pages of her book. 'This column shows how many letters come each month.'

The young man ran his finger down the column, hardly able to take in what he was reading. 'March 481, April 513, May 498, June 532, July 657, August 755!' He sat back, too amazed to speak.

'I wonder if Mrs Spurgeon will manage to keep the Book Fund going,' an elder at the church asked, after Charles died in January 1892. 'They were more in love than any couple I've ever known. She'll miss him most terribly.'

Susannah did miss Charles more than she

was ever able to put into words even to her twin sons who visited their mother nearly every day. But the Book Fund continued.

'When I think of how many books my darling husband needed for his work it makes me want to do even more for the poor men who can't afford to buy books,' she told a friend, not long before she died.

'Have you any idea how many ministers you've sent books to?' her companion asked.

Susannah smiled. 'Yes,' she said. 'I've always kept careful accounts and I can tell you that over 25,000 ministers have had books from the Book Fund, and all because Charles challenged me to make my wish come true.'

'What wish was that?' her friend asked.

'I wished that every minister could have a copy of his first book and he asked me what I'd do to make it happen. Since then I've just done what I could.'

Fact file: Queen Victoria.
During the life time of Charles and Susannah Spurgeon Queen Victoria was the ruling monarch of the British Empire. This was from 1837 until 1901. She was crowned Queen when she was only 18 years old. She married Prince Albert who, in 1851, organised the Great Exhibition. This was held in London and had more than 19,000 exhibits from all over the world. The venue was the Crystal Palace in Hyde Park - a building constructed from glass and iron. Many beautiful firework-displays were held there until it burnt down in 1936.

Keynote: Susannah Spurgeon didn't let her illness stop her working for God. Even though she couldn't get out of bed to see the cherry blossom the work she did for God went round the world. God can use anyone who loves and trusts in him to do great things for his Kingdom.

Susannah Spurgeon

Think: Susannah was amazed to see how God provided for the Book Fund. When she needed money to buy books the exact amount was sent. This proved to her that God was in charge of everything. Think about all the wonderful things God provides for you every day. Do you trust him to supply you with everything that you need? Is there a difference between what we want and what we need?

Prayer: Thank you, God, for everything you give me. Thank you for friends and family, food and drink, shelter and clothing. You care for all the things that my body needs. Thank you God for caring for my soul. Thank you so much for all the love you give to me and for saving me from my sin. Amen

Bethan Lloyd-Jones

Bethan felt very grown-up. 'This is exciting!' she told her eight-year-old brother, as they scrambled onto the train at Paddington Station in London. Dr Phillips climbed on behind them and put their luggage on the rack.

'Now you'll be good on the train,' Mrs Phillips said. 'Don't lean out of the window and don't go near the doors. When you reach Newcastle, Emlyn, your grandparents will be there to meet you.'

'You look after your brother,' Bethan's father said. 'And look after your little sister,' he added, smiling at Ieuan. 'It's time we got off,' he told his wife, 'or we'll be heading for Wales with them.'

The children looked out of the train window at their parents. Both were excited, but both had butterflies in their tummies. A whistle blew. Dr Phillips and his wife waved. There was a shudder. There was a judder. Then the train began to pull away from the platform. 'Goodbye! Goodbye!' the children shouted as they left. And Mrs Phillips discovered she was still waving after the train was well out of sight.

'You're very young to be travelling alone,' another passenger said to the children.

'I'm eight,' Ieuan told her, thinking that was really quite old.

'And I'm six,' announced Bethan, pulling herself up to be as big as she could possibly be.

'Are you going far?' the lady asked.

'We're going to our grandparents in Wales,' Bethan explained. 'There's a revival there and we're going to go to the meetings.'

'But it's not the school holidays,' commented the woman.

'My dad says we can go to school any day but we may never be able to go to a revival again,' Ieuan said.

'That may be true,' smiled the lady.

Ieuan went on, 'Dad says that this is a good year for the church in Wales and that a long time from now people will still talk about the Welsh Revival of 1904.'

The lady spoke to them again some time later. 'Do your parents always speak Welsh to you?' she asked, having heard them before they left London.

'We speak Welsh all the time at home,' Bethan said.

Bethan Lloyd-Jones

'How did you learn to speak such good English then?' was the next question.

Bethan explained that they had learned it at school.

'You're clever children,' smiled the lady.

The train chugged along and Bethan thought about home. 'I'll miss my baby brother while I'm in Wales,' she thought. 'Mum says he'll soon be crawling. I wonder if he'll learn to crawl while we're away.' She watched as the train went through the countryside and into a town. 'What's a revival like?' she wondered, as they passed a crowd of people at a market. 'Dad says there will be crowds there. And he says the singing will be wonderful.' As the blue-eyed little girl watched the world passing she twiddled her long dark hair.

Bethan found out that her father was right. She wrote home to tell her parents about it. 'The church is full for the meetings and people stand as well. Some even sit on windowsills and on the pulpit steps. A lot of people were crying last night. Grandad says that they were very sorry for the wrong things they had done.' Even when she was an old lady Bethan never forgot the Revival where hundreds of people came to believe in Jesus. 'Father was right to take us out of school and send us there,' she often thought. 'I wouldn't have liked to miss it.'

'Mum,' the girl said, when she was a teenager. 'I think we should call our home "The House of None-go-by" because it's always so full of people.' Her mother smiled.

'Well, your dad does have a habit of bringing people home with him.'

'But where does he find them all?' Bethan asked.

Mrs Phillips sat down. 'The Bible tells us to be hospitable, that means to make people welcome in our homes. And that's what we try to do. When Dad sees people needing help he brings them back here and we try to help them.'

Bethan laughed, 'Especially if they're Welsh! We've had Welsh tramps and Welsh alcoholics and sick Welsh people and sad Welsh people as well.'

Her mother laughed. 'The Welsh are special!' she said.

Bethan went out into their beautiful garden and sat on the swing. A young man walked up to her. He was using crutches. 'The peace of this place does me good,' he told the girl. 'I don't know what I'd have done if your parents hadn't taken me in.' Swinging slowly backwards and forwards she listened as he told his story. 'When I was injured in the War I'd nowhere to go and nobody to look after me. Dr Phillips heard about me and came to the hospital and brought me back here. He says I can stay until I find a room of my own and a job.'

'But there's no hurry to do that,' Bethan said.

The ex-soldier looked at the girl. 'She's just like her parents,' he thought. 'She'll always want to help people too.'

When Bethan was fifteen years old she met a boy called Martyn Lloyd-Jones at a church service. Fourteen years later, in January 1927, they were married. By then they had both trained to be doctors. But Bethan knew that she was not to be a doctor's wife. Martyn believed that God was calling him to preach. Soon after their marriage the newly-weds set out for Wales where Martyn was to be a minister in a church called Sandfields in Aberavon. Although Bethan was brought up in a Christian home and had always gone to church it was shortly after they moved to Wales that she really knew that she was a Christian.

'We enjoy the Women's Meetings so much,' a lady told Bethan one day. 'Could we have an evening Bible study as well?' Those standing around nodded their heads.

'I'll ask the Doctor,' Mrs Lloyd-Jones said.

'It's funny how she calls her husband

the Doctor,' a new girl to the congregation commented.

Her friend smiled. 'Everyone does.'

'He's quite happy for us to have an evening Bible study so long as it doesn't keep anyone away from the prayer meeting,' Bethan told the women after she'd discussed it with her husband. That was the beginning of a meeting that came to mean a lot to the girls and women of Sandfields.

'Mrs Lloyd-Jones is so easy to talk to,' a girl in the church told her friend. 'I'd a problem that was really getting me down and I didn't know who to go to for help. Then I thought of the Doctor's wife and she was great. Although she's so busy she didn't make me feel I was keeping her back from other things. And she gave me such good advice.'

Her friend smiled. 'You're not the first to go to her for help. And nobody's ever turned away.'

But it wasn't only the women of Sandfields that Bethan was able to help. As she sat at the back of the church one day a thin, grey-haired man with an amazing moustache appeared in church. 'Pray for him to be converted,' she was told. 'He's a wild man. He'll do anything for a fight. If he has a few drinks there's no stopping him.'

Bethan prayed.

'He's so bad that he always takes two of his buddies when he goes looking for a fight,' she was informed later.

'Why does he do that?' the minister's wife asked.

'So they can haul him off his victim when he's knocked him unconscious. Even McCann knows that he's liable to kill someone.'

On just the second Sunday the man was in church he became a Christian.

'It's a shame that McCann can't read,' a woman said to Bethan one evening as they left a meeting in the church hall.

'Can he not read?' she asked.

'Not a word. And it's a pity because now that he's a Christian he'd love to read the Bible.'

Mr McCann could hear what was being said, and Bethan noticed that he was hanging his head and shuffling his feet uncomfortably. 'Can you read anything at all?' she asked the new Christian gently.

'No,' he explained. 'I never learned. I didn't go to school much because I was always running away so I didn't ever learn to read.'

Bethan thought about Mark McCann and she remembered her childhood home. 'It can't be too difficult to teach an adult to read,' she thought. 'Mother taught a man in his seventies and they seemed to manage all right. And it's not all that difficult to learn, even small children do that!' These thoughts came and went in just a few seconds. 'I'm sure I can teach you to read if you would like to try,' she told the amazed Mr McCann. He jumped at the offer and they arranged a time for his first lesson.

'Let's start with this,' Bethan said, pointing to the words in her daughter's book The Little Red Hen. But not a single word would go into the man's head. The next lesson was the same and the next. As they settled down the following week Mark pushed The Little Red Hen away. 'I don't want to read about hens,' he said. 'I want to read the Bible.' Bethan reached for a Bible with good-sized print and opened it at John's gospel. Pointing with his finger Mark started with Jesus' words, 'I am the good shepherd.'

'It looks as though he might learn after all,' Bethan told the Doctor that evening. 'Either that or he has a good memory for words and he's not reading it at all.'

'I think he needs spectacles,' Mrs Lloyd-Jones said after one evening service. 'Mark's eyesight doesn't seem very good.'

'Trust a doctor to notice that!' someone commented.

Spectacles helped Mr McCann a lot – or so it seemed.

'Let's try something from Mark's gospel,' Bethan suggested. But when they turned the pages back to Mark the poor man couldn't read a single word!

'Funny, isn't it?' Mark McCann said. 'I can read John, but I can't read Mark, even though it's my own name!'

Bethan turned back to the book of John. 'Let's stick to this then,' she decided. And Mr McCann gradually learned to read his Bible.

'He's so excited about it,' people said. 'He just loves God's Word.'

Not long after her husband learned to read, Mrs McCann arrived at the Lloyd-Jones door. Mark was very ill and she wanted someone to visit him. As the Doctor was away Bethan went herself. She discovered that he was dying. But, in the weeks that followed, Mark McCann spent many hours with his new spectacles on, tracing the words of John's gospel with his finger and sounding them out one by one.

'I love meeting Mrs Lloyd-Jones,' a lady in Aberavon told her neighbour. 'When she asks how I am she really wants to know. It's not only my body, she wants to know how my soul is as well.'

The other woman nodded her head. 'So I've heard,' she said. 'But I doubt that she'd be interested in someone like me who doesn't go to the church at all.'

'She would if you needed her,' was the reply.

Suddenly the poor woman was in tears. 'If ever I needed help I need it now,' she wept.

The two neighbours went to church together the next Sunday and the woman was able to speak to Bethan. 'She was such a help,' sighed the relieved lady, as they walked home in the evening sun. But I hope she doesn't tell anyone what we talked about.'

Her neighbour shook her head. 'If you told Mrs Lloyd-Jones something private wild horses won't tear it out of her.'

After twelve years in Wales, Martyn and Bethan Lloyd-Jones moved with their two daughters to London. He was to be minister of a church there for the next thirty years.

'I don't know how we get people to go home after the service,' one of the men in the London congregation said, following an evening service not long after they moved. 'So many want to speak to the Doctor.'

His friend looked around the building and smiled.

'What's so funny?' he was asked. 'Just look at that,' his friend said. The two men turned round and looked at the queues of people. 'What do you see?'

'A whole line of people waiting to talk to the Doctor,' was the reply. Then the man broke into a wide smile. 'And an even longer queue waiting to talk to his wife!'

Just as he said those words, an elderly lady passed. 'I knew Mrs Lloyd-Jones' parents,' she told the two men. 'They always had time to speak to people and to try to help them. Bethan is exactly the same. What a difference people like her make by opening their hearts and homes.'

The lady walked slowly on. 'What she said is right enough,' one man said to the other. 'But Bethan Lloyd-Jones has done more than that. I heard her say once that her job was to keep her husband in the pulpit. And she's done that too. If she hadn't been there to look after him he'd have worn himself out years ago.'

Fact File: Welsh Language. The Welsh language is a Celtic language that has been spoken in Wales since about the time the Romans left Britain. Today Welsh is taught in schools throughout Wales even though English is used there more widely than in the past. Every year there is a festival in Wales called the Eisteddfod. Prizes are awarded for Welsh songs and poetry.

 Keynote: The revival that Bethan went to see happened in Wales in 1904-5. Revival is a time when Christians feel extra close to God and others come to believe in him. It is a special time. Revival can happen inside one person or inside many people at the same time. When God sends revival to Christians they become more enthusiastic about obeying him and telling others about him. If you are a Christian you should pray for a revival in your own life.

Think: Bethan parents loved to look after people and invite them into their home. This is called being hospitable. Hospitality is when someone shows love and care to a visitor in their home. The Bible tells us to be hospitable. You may not own or have a home of your own but you can always show love to someone new at school or in youth group and be hospitable in this way. When you are older and live in a home of your own you can show God's love to others by using your home to look after them.

Pray: Thank you, God, for my home. Help me to be loving and caring to all who visit it. Help me to tell them about you. Amen

Edith Schaeffer

Edith looked at the scrambled egg and toast that was put on the table for her tea. 'I don't want eggs,' she said. 'I want what my amah's having' (amah means nanny).

Mrs Seville looked at her five-year-old daughter. 'Chinese food is far too rich for you to have all the time. You can have it one day a week just now, and perhaps when you're six you can have it two days a week.'

The child thought about her mother's suggestion. 'That means I can have it every day by the time I'm twelve.'

Her mother smiled. 'Let's wait and see about that,' she said.

But although Edith ate her scrambled eggs she had her Chinese food, too, because she often visited the Chinese families in the mission compound just as they were sitting down to eat.

'Funny how she knows just when to come,' the local people said to each other. 'And she has good taste,' one of them commented, 'because she told me that our food looks nicer as well as tastes nicer than what she has at home.'

'Let's play at houses,' Edith suggested to her friend one morning. 'I'll be the mum and you can be the baby.'

For a while the game went well, then the baby grew fretful and started pretend crying.

'Sh, sh,' Edith said, patting her pal on the back. But the wailing grew louder and the patting harder. 'Shhh, shhhh,' roared the play mother. Her pretend daughter yelled at the top of her voice.

'Fichaw! Fichaw!' Edith screamed to make herself heard.

Mrs Seville, who had heard the racket, came running. Taking her daughter by the shoulders she looked right into her eyes. 'Don't let me hear you say that again!' she said firmly. Edith looked puzzled. 'That's not a polite thing to say.'

'But that's what my friends say,' the girl cried, 'and they don't get a row.'

Her mother smiled. 'I know they do,' she said. 'But it means shut up, and I'm sure you were telling your baby to be quiet, not to shut up!'

Edith's eyes sparkled as she thought that with all the wailing her pretend baby had been doing perhaps shut up was the right thing to say after all!

'There are disadvantages in being a working missionary mother,' Mrs Seville commented to her husband that evening. 'Although we dress as the Chinese do and you have your head shaved, apart from your pigtail, it's the girls who are most Chinese. It's just a pity that they pick up every slang expression they hear and don't seem interested in the polite ones!'

Her husband laughed. 'That's the price we pay for us both serving the Lord and relying on an amah to look after the girls.'

Mrs Seville smiled. 'It's a very small price. And it gives opportunities too. Even though Edith is just a little girl I often hear her telling her friends about Jesus. She seems to have a real gift for sitting down beside other children and just talking to them about the Lord.'

'I hope that's a gift she'll continue to use as she grows up,' her husband concluded. 'Then all her slang language will have been worth it.'

'It's today Elsa comes home,' Edith said excitedly.

'You miss your sister when she's away at school,' her amah nodded. 'What are you looking forward most to doing with her?'

The child knew without thinking what the answer was. 'We'll play Pilgrim's Progress.'

Amah laughed. 'That's been your favourite game since the very first time you heard the story.'

And before the day was out the game was well underway.

'You be Pilgrim,' Elsa told her little sister, as she handed her a pillowcase stuffed with things. Edith threw it over her shoulder. 'Now you climb up to the top of the hill on your hands and knees and leave your burden at the cross.'

Starting at the bottom of the stairs, Edith crawled up slowly, hauling her burden behind her. By the time she got to the top landing she really was glad to dump it down. 'The burden of sin has rolled off!' she yelled down the stairs to her sister.

Elsa clapped her hands, 'Hallelujah!' she shouted.

'I hate China!' Edith Seville announced soon afterwards. 'It's a cruel place.'

'I've never heard you say such a thing before,' her father replied, looking surprised and worried. 'What happened when you were out?'

The little girl rubbed her eyes to stop herself crying, but didn't manage. 'I was going in a rickshaw to my friend's house.

110

The coolie was running along when a little boy toddled out from the side of the road. The coolie saw him but he kept on running. I screamed but he just ran right over the little boy like he was rubbish on the street.'

'Was mother with you?' Mr Seville asked. 'Yes,' the girl wept, 'if she hadn't been there I'd have fallen out of the rickshaw. I was leaning so far out to see if the boy was all right.'

'Was he?' the man asked gently. Edith wiped the tears from her eyes.

'I don't know.'

Mr Seville put his arm around his young daughter. 'This world is a wonderful place,' he said, 'God saw to that. But we human beings can be cruel and hurtful and do terrible things. Let's hope that someone came along to lift up the child and look after him.'

'I wish I could have done that,' said Edith. 'I would have cuddled him better.'

'Let's do something really nice for a while,' Mrs Seville suggested, because her daughter was so upset. 'What would you like to do?'

Edith looked out the window. 'Could we take out my kites?' she asked.

Her mother smiled. 'You always choose to

do that when something's upsetting you.'

The pair of them took Edith's box kites to a little hill near the mission compound. Within minutes the kites were dancing above them, weaving in and out of each other, sometimes soaring high into the sky then diving towards the ground only to rise again like birds.

'This will do her good,' Mrs Seville thought. 'It's hard to be sad when you're flying a kite.'

After a wonderful half-hour the pair made their way home. Soon afterwards the Seville family left China and returned to America. It was 1919.

'What do you remember about China?' a friend asked Edith years later, when they were both students.

'I often think about my time there,' the girl replied, and then told her companion about the little boy who was knocked over and about her kites. 'And although I didn't see it, I knew that girl babies were sometimes so unwanted that they were left out to die. That upset me because I was a girl. I used to wonder what would have happened to me if I'd been born into a Chinese home.'

'It sounds an awful place,' her friend commented.

Edith thought for a minute. 'Terrible things did happen there, but it was such a strange mixture. There was great beauty and awful hurt. Even though I was a child when we left I still remember enjoying the beautiful things and wanting to cuddle everyone's hurts better.'

'And you've not changed a bit!' her friend said, thinking of the lovely little birthday present Edith had made for her, and of the times she'd been able to talk over her problems with her friend.

'Good morning, Mrs Schaeffer,' Francis said. 'How is my new wife this wonderful morning?' It was 1935, and Edith Seville and Francis Schaeffer had been married the previous day.

Edith grinned. 'Your wife is wonderfully well and wonderfully happy! Did we really get married yesterday or is this just a dream and I'm about to wake up and discover that you're not real at all?'

As they drove off on their honeymoon the young couple discussed their future.

'Remind me again how old you are.' Francis asked, although he knew already.

'I'm an old woman of twenty,' laughed Edith.

Her husband looked serious for a minute. 'I wonder what we'll be doing twenty years

113

from now. Will you still love me?'

'Yes,' Edith answered. 'I promised you that at our wedding!'

'And will we have a houseful of children?' he went on.

Edith leant over and gave Francis a kiss. 'Let's just wait and see,' she said.

Twenty years later was a time of great change in the Schaeffers' life. They stood outside a large Swiss chalet, looking up at the mountains around them, breathing in the clean air, and dreaming their dreams.

'L'Abri is a good name for this place,' Edith said. 'It means shelter, and I hope it will be a shelter to those who come to stay with us here.'

'There's some work to be done before it's fit for anyone,' Francis laughed, 'apart from our own four children of course.'

'Let's go look see,' his wife suggested. They went from room to room.

'That ceiling will need repaired,' Francis said, looking at some cracks.

'And those pot-bellied stoves really must come out,' said Edith.

'We could drape curtains on that wall.' 'Those light shades looks as though they've been chewed!' 'This floor is dangerously uneven.' 'Ugh! I couldn't live with that colour of paint!' There seemed to be no end of things to do.

'Do you hope to make L'Abri a conference centre?' one of their new neighbours asked.

Edith thought for a moment. 'No,' she replied. 'It's going to be a home – our home – and we'll share it with whoever comes.'

The neighbour looked up at the chalet and thought of all the work that was being done on it, mostly by the Schaeffers themselves. 'You must be expecting a lot of important people,' he said.

'Everyone who comes will be important,' Edith smiled. 'Even if nobody else thinks so.'

'What do you mean?' enquired the neighbour.

'Everyone is important to God,' Edith explained. 'We hope that this house will be a place where people can find quietness and healing and also the peace of God.'

'How do you do that?' her friend asked.

The heavy rucksack the man carried reminded Edith of her childhood game of Pilgrim's Progress. She told him that Jesus had died to take away the burden of sin, and that when she asked his forgiveness God had given her his gift of peace.

'Are you sure I'll be welcome at L'Abri?' Sarah asked her university friend.

'I'm certain,' was the answer. 'Everybody's

welcome at L'Abri.' And when the pair arrived Sarah discovered how true that was. She wrote home to her sister, 'What a place this is! There are people everywhere. Francis Schaeffer answers questions all the time: by the fire, round the barbecue, even when we're out walking. And the questions! You have no idea the hard things that are discussed here. I had lots of questions myself when I came. I just didn't understand what the Bible was all about. But when I listen to Francis Schaeffer, I feel I'm beginning to understand. Perhaps by the time I leave I'll believe in Jesus. The longer I stay the more I want that to be true.'

'You wrote about Francis Schaeffer,' Sarah's sister said, after the girl had returned home. 'What about his wife? What's she like?'

A smile crossed Sarah's face. 'At first I couldn't work out what she did,' the girl explained. 'Then I realised what an amazing woman she is. While her husband answered difficult questions she cared for people's problems. If my heart were breaking Edith Schaeffer would be the person I'd go to. Not only that,' Sarah went on, 'but she spread beauty all around her. Every room had wild flowers and welcome notes in it. Even though there are so many people coming and going, Edith Schaeffer makes L'Abri a home, not a conference centre.'

'She sounds like my kind of person,' her sister concluded.

The two girls walked along the road towards their home. 'Did the Schaeffers make you feel you had to become a Christian?' Sarah's sister asked.

'No,' was the reply. 'Absolutely not. We were able to ask all the questions that worried us, but that was all.'

'And did you become a Christian?'

'Yes,' Sarah stopped and smiled at her sister. 'Yes I did. But do you know something? It wasn't because Francis Schaeffer answered my questions - it was because Edith Schaeffer loved me. And I'm sure there are hundreds of people who have become Christians because God has used the pair of them.'

Her sister looked interested. 'I've got lots of questions myself,' she announced. 'Could we go to L'Abri together next summer?'

Sarah grinned from ear to ear. 'Try to stop us,' she said.

L'Abri has now spread beyond Switzerland, and although Francis and Edith Schaeffer have now gone to heaven, there are people in centres in several countries who continue the work they started.

Fact File: Kite Flying. Kite flying is a very popular pass-time in the Far East. In China the ninth day of the ninth month is a kite-flying festival when grown-ups as well as children go out to fly kites. Sometimes there are kite-flying competitions where kite owners try to cut the cords of other kites. The winner is the first one to cut another kite's cord. When the kite falls to the ground the winner can keep it for himself.

Keynote: When Edith and Francis started 'L'Abri' they wanted everyone to feel welcome there. Anyone who wanted to come and stay with them could do just that. Everybody who came was important - no one was looked down on. It is good to treat people fairly. Jesus was friends with rich and poor people. We should be the same.

Think: Edith used to play a game when she was little in which she would pretend that a great big sack on her shoulder was the burden of sin. It was only Jesus who could get rid of the burden of sin. Sin can be a burden to us because it makes our lives miserable. We need to get rid of it or it will be impossible for us to enter heaven. Jesus is the only one who can get rid of our sins for us. He can do this because he died on the cross instead of us.

Prayer: Thank you, God, for forgiveness of sins. I am sorry for disobeying you. Help me to love you and obey you more each day. Amen.

Sabina Wurmbrand

Sabina watched as her mother lit the candles one by one until all seven flickered into life. This was the time of the week the girl loved best. 'We're all here,' she told her mother.

Mrs Oster smiled, 'And on good time for the Sabbath meal.' The smell of chicken livers cooking wafted through from the kitchen, mingling with the warmth of new-baked bread.

'Come now,' Mr Oster said, 'the Sabbath meal is ready.' The large family sat down around the table, with the light of seven candles reflecting in all their eyes. Sabina's father prayed, and in the silence that followed she thought about all the other Jewish families in Romania who were gathering for their Sabbath meals.

The meal over, the seven-year-old curled in the corner of a couch where she could watch her father. He stood at the window, his skull-cap on the back of his head and his prayer shawl draped over his shoulders. She watched as he fingered the fringes that hung from it, swaying backwards and forwards as he did so.

Mr Oster wasn't exactly singing, but from somewhere deep inside himself came the sound of a melody that reached back hundreds of years.

Sabina thought about her grandfather and great grandfather who had said the same words. Sabina wondered if one day she would have sons who would say the same words in the same way?

'Are you praying, Papa?' the girl asked. Her words seemed to take time to come to her father's attention.

'Yes,' he said eventually, 'I'm praying.'

'Who are you praying for, Papa?' she went on.

Slowly Mr Oster turned round to face his daughter and the other members of the family. 'I'm praying for our fathers and mothers, for our brothers and sisters, and for our children and our children's children.'

Sabina looked puzzled. 'But your children don't have any children,' she queried.

Her father's face took on a faraway look. 'Every Jew prays for his children's children,' he explained. 'It's part of the promise.'

As soon as she opened her eyes the next morning Sabina knew it was the Sabbath by the heat in the room. 'That's nice,' she thought, snuggling her dressing-gown around her. 'Imagine how cold it must be in Gentile houses this morning,' she said, looking out the window at the snow. 'They've got to wait until their fires are cleared out and lit before they have any heat. Because we don't work on the Sabbath our fire is kept on all night and our home is lovely and warm.'

'Papa,' the girl said, when her father came home from the synagogue, 'why do Jews not have a Christmas?'

Mr Oster's face coloured. 'Can a seven-year-old use that word and ask a question like that?'

It was Sabina's turn to blush. She knew that she couldn't say the word 'Christ', and she'd not realized that by saying 'Christmas' she'd broken that rule.

'This is the time of year when Gentiles celebrate the coming of the Messiah. But they're badly wrong. The Messiah has not yet come. We are still in the days of waiting for God's Promised One. The one they celebrate at this time of year is a man, and one who broke the Law at that.' Sabina looked shocked. 'Their so-called messiah was put to death for acting as though he

123

was Jehovah himself.'

Mr Oster draped his prayer shawl round his shoulders and stood looking out the window. It was as though he could see to the farthest parts of the world. His fingers seemed to number the fringes, and then the low sound began inside him. It grew gradually louder until the room seemed full of the noise of it. As she listened Sabina felt a very special connection to her people, the Jews, and for the first time she began to understand about children's children. The melody of her father's prayer flowed through her. What would the future bring for her and her children, she wondered, as her father's prayer drew to a close.

Sabina learned when to ask her father questions and when not to. 'Sometimes the look in his eyes hurts so much that I can't interrupt it,' she thought, wondering what the hurt was about. 'And other times, though not often nowadays, Papa's eyes look like sunshine and then I can ask him anything.'

She watched and waited for his sunshine eyes. One day, when her father's eyes were shining, Sabrina asked the question. She was nearly sixteen, and she knew she had to ask.

'Why are Jews such a sad people, Papa? We have the promise of the Messiah to look forward to, yet there is a deep sadness inside us.'

It was as though shutters slammed over her father's eyes, as though a brick had hit him, as though a great burden was bending his back. 'Sit down,' he said. And she did.

By the time Sabina stood up again she was helping to carry the burden. She had learned the secret of Jewish sadness and felt that it would never let her go.

'I just can't take it in,' she thought, as she tossed and turned in bed all night. 'The man called Jesus broke Jehovah's Law; that's why they crucified him. How can it be that nearly two thousand years later people hate the Jews for putting him to death when it was his own fault? How can people hate me for what happened all that time ago? How can they hate my children's children?'

'We're living in a nightmare,' Sabina told her boyfriend, Richard. 'Jews are being persecuted throughout Eastern Europe.'

'Forget it,' he said. 'I want us to forget we're Jews and enjoy ourselves. What will we do tonight? The pictures? A walk? A drink?'

Sabina shook herself. 'OK,' she said. 'Let's forget the world. Let's go for a drink then find a film.'

Richard grinned. 'Anything for you!'

Perhaps it was a romantic film that made them think of wedding bells - for Richard Wurmbrand and Sabina were married in 1936.

When Sabina married, she no doubt assumed that her family life would be much as hers had been. After all, she had married a Jew, a man from the same background as herself. But that was not to be. Before long Richard became interested in the Christian faith. That was bad enough, but what followed was to his new young wife quite shocking.

'A Christian!' Sabina breathed, too shocked to say the word louder. 'But a Jew can't become a Christian,' she whispered, swallowing every time she used the word with Christ in it. 'If you do, that's the end of our marriage and our love.' It didn't matter what Richard tried to say, or how tender and loving he was, it was as though their marriage had died. He tried every way he could think of to interest Sabina in his newly-found faith, but he hit a stone wall every time. Then he had an idea.

'Would you like to go to the pictures?' he asked brightly one night. Sabina looked surprised then agreed. Richard took her to the most disgusting film that was on, and stayed until Sabina was sick of it.

'Want to party?' he asked. His wife thought that would be an improvement on the film they'd seen. But she was wrong. Very cunningly Richard had done his homework and he took her to a party where people were horribly drunk and awful things were happening.

'Let's go home,' Sabina begged.

'Not at all,' he laughed.

'Please!' she hissed. 'Let's get out of here.' These outings brought the young woman to her senses. She realised that what she'd seen had been life without God, and she knew from the change in her husband that the God who made a difference was the Lord Jesus Christ. Sabina Wurmbrand became a Christian. It's hard to imagine how her family and friends must have felt when she told them that she believed that Jesus was the Messiah.

It was 1943, the Second World War was raging, and Romanian Jews were being deported to Nazi concentration camps.

'You're so thin,' Richard said sadly, looking at what seemed like just a shadow of the girl he'd married. He put his arm around Sabina and steered her to a chair.

'How much more can happen?' she asked. 'How much more?' She shuddered. 'My parents, my sisters and my brother all dead, all dead in the camps,' she said weakly. 'Why did the Nazis kill them? Why?'

'May God forgive them,' prayed Richard. Sabina looked at him and nodded.

'May God forgive them,' she repeated. 'And I'll pray that prayer over and over again until I mean it with all my heart.' And that's exactly what Sabina Wurmbrand did.

'Let me introduce you,' the editor of the most popular newspaper in Romania said to the men on either side of him the following year. 'Richard, this is Stephen, Stephen, meet Richard.'

Stephen held out his hand. 'Well am I pleased to meet you!' he said. 'I've heard so much about you and your wife.'

Wurmbrand smiled. 'She's quite a woman,' he said.

'Our friend here has told me about the work you do,' Stephen commented. 'But I'd really like to hear about your wife's work.'

'How long have you got?' laughed Richard, having had a nod from the newspaper editor assuring him that it was safe to talk. They sat down together in the soundproofed newspaper office.

'Sabina has had a busy war,' Richard began. 'She's smuggled many Jewish children out of the ghettos. Every day she preaches to the people gathered in bomb shelters. She and I have helped start the Jewish-Christian Church. And she's one of the

Romanian underground's most enthusiastic workers. If this war is won,' he concluded, 'it will be won by the likes of my wife. My job is to preach the gospel, her job is very much more hands-on helping.'

'How have the pair of you kept out of prison?' Stephen asked. Richard nodded in the direction of the editor. 'Thanks to my good friend here,' he explained. 'Although we've been arrested several times he's managed to say a word for us where it matters.'

Communism settled its grey cloud on Europe after the Second World War and Sabina did what she could to help those who were caught in the poverty that followed.

'What's the programme for this week?' Richard asked most Mondays. 'Helping in the soup kitchen,' she replied sometimes. 'Smuggling food to refugees.' 'Trying to get salt to Budapest.' 'I must get on with planning the camp for religious leaders.'

Each time he asked the question the answer seemed to be different. 'Life's not boring,' he commented from time to time.

Sabina looked up. 'Boredom? What does that feel like?' she grinned.

'It's 1948,' Sabina wrote in her diary, 'and everybody outside Europe thinks the

War is over and peace has broken out. But the only thing that's broken today is my heart. Richard has disappeared! Little Mihai is crying for his daddy. How can a boy understand that his daddy has disappeared? Someone told me that he was lifted off the street and driven away. But where? And for how long?' The waiting time had begun.

'Your husband has gone and left you!' two members of the secret police told Sabina, some months later. 'Divorce him and forget he ever existed.' She looked at Mihai. 'Can I forget my husband?' she asked. 'Should I forget my son's father?' 'Think about it,' one of the men said, trying to sound kind, 'we'll give you time to think about it.'

Clocks all over Romania ticked the minutes away, days full of minutes, months full of minutes, and years full of thousands of minutes.

'Divorce him!' the secret policeman hissed. 'He doesn't exist any longer. Divorce him and give your child a new father.'

Sabina and Mihai's eyes met. 'Richard will hardly recognise him. Mihai has grown such a lot in the last three years,' she thought, then said aloud, 'I will never divorce my husband.'

The man turned on his heels and stomped towards the door. 'You're running out of time!' he growled as he left.

'I thank God for that,' Sabina told her son. 'Every day that passes we are nearer seeing your father again on earth or in heaven.' But Sabina Wurmbrand didn't spend her time idly waiting even though the authorities refused to allow her to work. She was as busy as ever helping Jews and spreading the gospel and encouraging Christian people to keep on believing whatever happened to them.

'You'll take me away from my son?' Sabina asked, horrified.

'You've brought it on yourself,' she was told. 'Now you'll pay for your stubbornness.'

She did, with three years' hard labour. 'They can do what they like to me,' she often thought, as she worked on building a canal, 'but they can't stop me praying.' And as she loaded box-cars with stones she prayed, 'Father, forgive them. And be with Richard and Mihai, hold them close to yourself.'

In the fifteen years following her release Sabina worked to help both Jews and Gentiles, and Mihai grew to be a young man. From time to time they heard news of Richard, but the last they heard was that he was dead. For the first time in all their years apart Sabina believed it.

'Mum! What's wrong?' Mihai yelled, as

Sabina slumped to the floor some time later. She had collapsed as she answered the phone. The shock of hearing Richard's voice was too much for her. Completely out of the blue he had been released from hospital prison. And a little time later, looking just like skin and bone, he arrived on their doorstep. That was the beginning of the end of Sabina's lonely journey and the start of their work together to tell the West about the reality of Communism as well as helping the persecuted church world-wide.

Fact File: Ghetto. This word is used today to describe an area in a city where one group of people or a nationality live. The word was originally used hundreds of years ago to describe an area of a city where Jewish people lived. During the 2nd World War Jewish people were once again forced to live in ghettos. The Nazi government under Adolf Hitler would not allow Jewish people to live with other nationalities. These ghettos were not safe as the Nazis would often raid them in order to capture Jews and take them off to concentration camps. Men and women like Richard and Sabina Wurmbrand did all they could to help these people escape.

Keynote: Sabina realised that her husband Richard had changed for the better because of Jesus Christ. Jesus Christ has the power to cleanse you from all your sin and change your life for the better too.

Think: Sabina forgave her enemies - even those who had killed her family. Jesus tells us to love our enemies. Would you love your enemies? Do you find it hard to forgive? If you do, ask Jesus to help you.

Prayer: Lord Jesus, thank you for being my friend. Help me to love other people and treat them in a way that I would want to be treated. Give me the strength to love those who hate me. Forgive me for my sin and help me to forgive others. Amen

Ruth Bell Graham

Wang Nai Nai called to the little girl to wave goodbye to her dad who was going off to work in the hospital. The child came running, waved till there was no longer any sight of her dad, then gave her amah a hug. These two, a Chinese woman and an American child, loved each other. Ruth, when she looked at her amah, saw a face so lined with laughter that it was beautiful. Others also saw lines caused by the hardship of many generations of poverty and things that the child was far too young to understand. There were no lines on Ruth's face apart from when she screwed up her eyes in the sunlight and when she looked into Wang Nai Nai's twinkling eyes there was nothing at all to trouble her.

A second girl ran into the room and was caught in her amah's arms.

'Where were you?' Wang Nai Nai asked. 'You didn't come when I called you to wave to your dad.'

'I'm sorry,' Rosa said. 'I didn't hear you.'

The woman nodded. 'Let me guess,' she said. 'You were reading a book.'

Rosa grinned and nodded. 'It's a good book too.'

'I've never met a family like the Bells for reading books. And when you read you seem to leave the world behind and go into the world of your story book.'

'That's an idea!' Rosa said, clapping her hands in excitement. 'Let's play at Alice in Wonderland.'

Ruth's eyes shone. 'You be Alice, Rosa, and Amah, you can be the Mad Hatter.'

There was no response from Wang Nai Nai, and when the girls eventually tracked her down to her bedroom they knew they would have to do without the Mad Hatter, because their amah was sitting on a low stool singing from a book of Chinese hymns that had been carefully bound together by hand.

'She can be the Queen of Hearts,' Rosa whispered, as they went downstairs, 'because she doesn't come into the story for a while.'

'Mummy,' both girls said together. 'Can we please have clothes from the barrel to play with?'

Mrs. Bell looked at her daughters. 'You are both growing so quickly I was thinking we'd have to look in the barrel anyway.'

Rosa and Ruth had a happy morning going through a barrelful of clothes, deciding what could be used for Alice in Wonderland and what the girls had grown into.

It was only after the barrel was repacked that Mrs Bell realized Ruth was looking sad. 'What's the matter?' she asked the seven-year-old.

Ruth tried to explain. 'All the Chinese people wear pretty colours and shiny material and our clothes are never as nice.'

Mrs. Bell pulled Ruth on to her knee with one arm and put her other arm round Rosa. 'People back home in America are very kind to missionaries such as ourselves,' she said. 'They give money for doctors like Dad and they pay for all the things in the hospital too. Not only that, but they keep their children's best clothes after they have outgrown them and send them half-way round the world so that you can have good warm clothes to wear in the cold climate of China. It's really very kind of them.'

'I know that,' Ruth told her mum. 'But sometimes I'd like a new dress of my own.'

Wang Nai Nai came into the room, 'I'm ready to be the Queen of Hearts,' she announced. Ruth, forgetting all about new dresses, set her mind on being the Mad Hatter.

Saying good-bye was something Ruth got used to doing. Each day she waved to her father as he left the mission house to go to work in the hospital. Other missionaries came and went over the years and each had to be welcomed and waved good-bye.

There was a time when the Bells waved to their Chinese friends, especially Wang Nai Nai, as they left for a trip to America. But even saying good-bye to her amah was not as hard as what was to come.

When Ruth was twelve years old, Rosa was sent away to the Pyeng Yang Foreign School in North Korea. For a whole year Ruth tried to push out of her mind the thought that she would soon be going to join her sister. But it wouldn't go away. She begged her parents to allow her to stay at home with them in China. Many nights she cried herself to sleep. And the night before she left for school she prayed that she would die before morning. She didn't.

On 2nd September 1933, thirteen-year-old Ruth was one of five missionary children who climbed on board the Nagasake Maru that was berthed in the Whangpoo River. She felt as though her heart would break as the gangway was dragged on board the boat then the ropes were loosened on the quayside. And when the vessel creaked into motion and edged into the muddy midstream she knew that childhood was behind her, and happiness too. Ruth Bell didn't believe that away from her parents, apart from her amah, and outside of China she could find any happiness at all.

'There's the Yangtze!' one of the children shouted, as they came to where the muddy Whangpoo joined the even muddier great Yangtze River. There were excited runnings and shoutings, but nothing stirred in Ruth. It was the same when the Yangtze flowed into the East China Sea. Each landmark made Ruth more miserable, and she thought her misery was complete when she eventually arrived at the Pyeng Yang School.

For a time she was so utterly homesick it was as though she was split in two, her heart in China and her body in North Korea. It was only when she became ill and had to spend some time in the school infirmary that Ruth found any comfort at all, and that was because she spent her time there reading the psalms in the Bible. Although she was just thirteen years old she read all one hundred and fifty psalms.

At first it surprised Ruth to read that King David, who wrote most of the psalms, had sometimes felt miserable too. As she read on she was comforted to discover that God had been with King David in his miserable times and he was with her too.

Four years later, Ruth, having finished school, was again being bundled off on a journey. It was 1937. Japan had attacked China near Beijing and Japanese forces were beginning to overrun the northern part of the country.

Dr Bell, convinced that there was going to be war, was doing what he could in the hospital to prepare for it. Mrs Bell was busy too, packing and repacking Ruth's belongings for her to sail to America where she was to attend Wheaton College. And Ruth? She was sure of two things: that she would never marry and that God wanted her to be a missionary. 'So why,' she asked her mother as they folded her clothes, 'do I need to go all the way to college in America?'

The Bells were delighted with what their daughter wanted to do with her life but they still put her on a ship for America, knowing that she had a lot to learn and that college would do her good.

The kind of freedom Ruth had at college was completely new to her, and she made such good use of it that she was nearly asked to leave just a few weeks after she arrived! The authorities didn't appreciate her coming in so late that the doors were locked. And they liked it even less that she climbed in her bedroom window rather than knock and wait for the door to be opened! Ruth was given the choice of being expelled or grounded. She chose to be grounded. Had she been expelled she would never have met William (Billy) Franklin Graham, a young Baptist minister who arrived to study at the same college.

'Billy's six foot two at least,' one of Ruth's friends told her.

'And he's twenty-one years old,' said another.

'He's from North Carolina,' Ruth added, 'and he's already a minister.'

One girl smiled dreamily. 'Have you seen his eyes?' she asked. 'They are the clearest bluest eyes I've ever seen.'

It was no wonder he had plenty of girlfriends!

But before long there was one special girl in Billy's life. He and Ruth Bell made a wonderful pair. Although Ruth had thought she would never be married, as soon as she knew Billy Graham she was sure he was the young man God meant for her. And on 13th August 1943, William Franklin Graham and Ruth Bell became man and wife.

After all the good-byes Ruth had said in her life it was a relief to her to feel the time had come to settle down with the man she loved, to build up a home, to have children. She could picture in her mind what

her future might be like. They would have a
comfortable home and a friendly church. As
Ruth felt that Billy was a gifted preacher,
she pictured him taking meetings all around
the area. But he'd be at home in his study
each morning, she thought. That would be
lovely if God gave us children, though they
would have to be quiet outside his study
and not disturb him. He would be there
for the children; he'd be there for her. As
Ruth sewed curtains for their first home
it was as though she was stitching dreams
together.

'It's a wonderful opportunity,' Billy told
his wife, two years later. 'Evangelism is
what's in my heart and this would let me do
it full time.'

'We could move near Dad and Mum,' Ruth
said. 'It would be so good to be nearer them
now that they've retired back to America.'

They prayed about it, talked about it,
worked out all the details, and decided that
Billy should give up being a regular minister
and become a full-time evangelist. What
Ruth had perhaps not realised was that
she was signing away her dream of an at-
home husband and father. As time passed
Billy's preaching trips took him further and
further away, more and more often. Ruth,
who had thought she had said good-bye

to good-byes, now regularly found herself waving to her husband as he left, yet again, with his suitcase in one hand and his coat trailing from the other.

Billy and Ruth Graham had five children, three daughters and two sons. Gigi, Anne, Bunny, Franklin and Ned grew up with a dad who became better known every year. He was on radio and television and had books written about him too. But to his sons and daughters he wasn't Billy Graham, the world famous preacher; he was Dad.

They loved it when he was home, enjoying the rough and tumble, the stories he told of faraway places and interesting people, of strange food eaten in strange places. And when he went away they knew that Mum would be quiet for a day then go into busy mode to keep her mind off the good-bye.

'Why don't you travel with Dad?' the children asked her often, after they had grown up a bit.

'It's not for me,' she explained, 'though you know I've gone some places with Dad. My job is to keep the nest warm here for all of you and for him when he comes back home.'

'This is a bit like a nest,' one of the girls told Ruth. It was a bright sunny day and they were sitting outside their cabin home, surrounded by trees in Little Piney

Cove. 'The cabin kind of nestles here, and because so much of it is wooden I can almost imagine it's on the branch of a great tree,' the teenager went on.

Ruth thought about what she was hearing. 'I'm glad you feel like that,' she said. 'Because that's what I set out to do here, to make a nest for the Grahams, to make a nest for your Dad.'

'You've never got used to Dad being away so much, have you?' the girl asked.

Ruth thought before answering. 'It's our way of life,' she said carefully, 'and God has given us both the strength to be often apart but still to love each other so much. But no, I've never really got used to partings.'

'Mum,' her daughter said, feeling somehow that Ruth was in a sharing mood, 'you once said that you thought God wanted you to be a missionary. But you're not, are you?'

Ruth smiled at the teenager, and thought how she was growing up. 'I am,' she said, 'because the Lord has allowed me to talk to many people about Jesus. But I think my missionary service has been to agree to your Dad's preaching trips. I often had to say good-bye as a girl and it was always hard. Now I realise that was part of my training for being Billy Graham's wife.'

'I suppose that's right,' the girl agreed. 'Because if you'd insisted that Dad settled down to work in one church he'd not have told millions of people about the Lord.'

Ruth's eyes were closed against the glare of the sun. 'It's amazing really,' she said softly, as if to herself, 'he has preached in over sixty countries, even in Communist Russia, and he's told millions and millions of people the good news that Jesus is the Saviour.'

'So it's been worth it?' her daughter asked.

Ruth was instantly upright and wide awake. 'Worth it?' she said. 'Of course it's been worth it. Not easy ... but worth every single painful good-bye.'

The girl got up and poked the charcoal on the barbecue. 'Just nine more days till Dad comes home now,' she said.

Ruth laughed. 'Now where's my list?' she asked. 'I'll have to remember to get his favourite hot chocolate and popcorn and ...'

'It's OK Mum!' her daughter said, grinning, 'you've got a whole nine days to get all his favourites ready before you welcome him back to the nest, and you've started to flutter already!'

Fact File: Yangtze River. The Yangtze River is China's greatest river and fourth longest river in the world. It flows for 5,494 kilometres from its source in Tibet to the point it enters the East China Sea. The Explorer Marco Polo once mentioned how impressed he was with the number of boats using the river. But nowadays heavy rains in summer sometimes cause disastrous flooding.

Keynote: Ruth was upset when she had to leave her parents in order to go to school. She was depressed and very home-sick. However, she read the Book of Psalms and found that other people understood what she was going through. It also made her realise that God was with her. When you feel down and depressed pray to God, ask him to give you comfort in his Word the Bible.

Think: Ruth and Billy were both involved in evangelism. Evangelism is telling others about Jesus Christ. You can evangelise anywhere you go. You can evangelise in other countries, in other cities and you can also evangelise in your own home. Telling the people you know and love that Jesus wants to save them from sin is very important. But we are also told by Jesus to go into all the world to preach the gospel.

Prayer: Lord, you are amazing and wonderful. You are the God of love. You are the only true God. Help me to tell others about you and to do my bit to spread the good news around the whole world. Amen

Quiz

How much can you remember about these ten girls who made a difference? Try answering these questions to find out.

Monica of Thagaste

1. Monica grew up in a town in North Africa. What was its name?

2. What was the name of Monica's son?

3. Which country did Monica move to when she left Africa?

Katherine Luther

4. What was Katherine's last name before she married Martin Luther?

5. What did Katherine become when she was sixteen years old?

6. How many children at one point were living in Katherine and Martin's home?

Susanna Wesley

7. How many older brothers and sisters did Susanna have?

8. Who did Susanna eventually marry?

9. What happened to Susanna's home in 1709?

Ann Judson

10. What country did Ann travel to?

11. What was the name of Ann's husband?

12. What did Ann hide inside a pillow and smuggle into a prison?

Maria Taylor

13. Which country did Maria have to travel to when she was a child?

14. What hair-do did Hudson wear?

15. What was the name of Maria and Hudson's little girl?

Susannah Spurgeon

16. Which book did Charles give Susannah before they were married?

17. What presents did Susannah ask Charles to get her one day?

18. What did Susannah send to ministers who earned less than £150 a year?

Bethan Lloyd-Jones

19. What did Bethan and her brother go to see when Bethan was only six years old?

20. Which two languages did Bethan speak when she was a little girl?

21. What job did Bethan's husband Martyn do?

Edith Schaeffer

22. Which country did Edith live in as a young girl?

23. What did Edith like to do most when she was feeling sad?

24. Which country did Edith and Francis move to when they set up their new home, 'L'Abri'?

Sabina Wurmbrand

25. Which name was Sabina not allowed to say when she was a child?

26. Which country did Sabina live in?

27. What did the communists do to Sabina's husband Richard?

Ruth Bell Graham

28. Where did Ruth and Rosa get their clothes from?

29. What part of the Bible did Ruth read when she felt very homesick?

30. What did Ruth's husband, Billy Graham become after he was a pastor?

How well did you do?
Turn over to find out.

Answers:

1. Thagaste.
2. Augustine.
3. Italy.
4. von Bora.
5. A nun.
6. 17 (6 of their own and 11 orphans).
7. 24.
8. Samuel Wesley.
9. It burnt down.
10. Burma.
11. Adoniram.
12. The Burmese translation of the Bible.
13. England.
14. A Chinese pigtail.
15. Grace.
16. The Pilgrim's Progress.
17. An opal ring and a bullfinch.
18. Books.
19. The Welsh revivals of 1904-05.
20. Welsh and English.
21. A Preacher.
22. China.
23. Fly kites.
24. Switzerland.
25. Jesus Christ.

26. Romania.
27. They put him in prison.
28. A missionary barrel.
29. The Psalms.
30. An evangelist.

Start collecting this series now!

Ten Boys who used their Talents:
ISBN 978-1-84550-146-4
Paul Brand, Ghillean Prance, C.S.Lewis,
C.T. Studd, Wilfred Grenfell, J.S. Bach,
James Clerk Maxwell, Samuel Morse,
George Washington Carver, John Bunyan.

Ten Girls who used their Talents:
ISBN 978-1-84550-147-1
Helen Roseveare, Maureen McKenna,
Anne Lawson, Harriet Beecher Stowe,
Sarah Edwards, Selina Countess of Huntingdon,
Mildred Cable, Katie Ann MacKinnon,
Patricia St. John, Mary Verghese.

Ten Boys who Changed the World:
ISBN 978-1-85792-579-1
David Livingstone, Billy Graham, Brother Andrew,
John Newton, William Carey, George Müller,
Nicky Cruz, Eric Liddell, Luis Palau,
Adoniram Judson.

Ten Girls who Changed the World:
ISBN 978-1-85792-649-1
Corrie Ten Boom, Mary Slessor,
Joni Eareckson Tada, Isobel Kuhn,
Amy Carmichael, Elizabeth Fry, Evelyn Brand,
Gladys Aylward, Catherine Booth, Jackie Pullinger.

Ten Boys who Made a Difference:
ISBN 978-1-85792-775-7
Augustine of Hippo, Jan Hus, Martin Luther,
Ulrich Zwingli, William Tyndale, Hugh Latimer,
John Calvin, John Knox, Lord Shaftesbury,
Thomas Chalmers.